the little book of Angels

the little book of Angels

welcome angels into your life

vanessa lampert

CICO BOOKS

First published in 2026 by CICO Books
an imprint of Ryland Peters & Small Ltd
20–21 Jockey's Fields
London WC1R 4BW
www.rylandpeters.com
Email: euregulations@rylandpeters.com

Text adapted from *The Angel Book*, first published in 2007

10 9 8 7 6 5 4 3 2 1

See page 144 for illustration credits.

A CIP record for this book is available from the British Library.
US Library of Congress CIP data has been applied for.

ISBN: 978-1-80065-667-3

Printed in China

Editor: Marion Paull
Commissioning editor: Kristine Pidkameny
Desk editor: Imogen Valler-Miles
Senior designer: Emily Breen
Production manager: Gordana Simakovic
Publishing manager: Carmel Edmonds

The authorised representative in the EEA is
Authorised Rep Compliance Ltd.,
Ground Floor. 71 Lower Baggot Street,
Dublin, D01 P593, Ireland
www.arccompliance.com

FSC
www.fsc.org
MIX
Paper | Supporting responsible forestry
FSC® C106563

SAFETY NOTES

Neither the author nor the publisher can be held responsible for any claim arising out of the general information and practices provided in this book. While the use of particular practices may refer to healing benefits, they are not intended to replace diagnosis of illness or ailments, or healing or medicine. Always consult your doctor or other health professional in the case of illness. The safe and proper use of candles and incense is the sole responsibility of the person using them. Never burn a flame on or near anything that might catch fire and do not leave unattended. Keep out of the reach of children and pets and ensure good ventilation.

CONTENTS

INTRODUCTION

This book is a celebration of angels. It starts by introducing you to what angels are, and provides a fascinating account of angels throughout history, documenting their influence worldwide and across religions. You will learn about the different groups of angels, including archangels, such as Gabriel and Raphael, guardian angels, and even fallen angels. You will find out which aspects of your life angels can help you with and explore the ways in which you can open yourself up to angelic contact. You will discover how angels can communicate with you, which will enable you to become aware

of the presence of these powerfully protective beings and hear their messages. You will then be introduced to simple practices for letting angels into your life—using meditations, colors, candles, crystals, and more. Finally, you will learn the many ways in which angels can support and guide you through every stage of your life and help you to work through everyday challenges, from tackling relationship problems and low self-esteem, to coping with grief and bad news. The "angel messages" included at the end of each chapter will deepen your angelic connection.

CHAPTER 1

All About Angels

The word "angel" comes from the Greek "angelos," which means "messenger." The corresponding Hebrew word is "mal'ak," which has the same meaning. Angels are celestial beings of pure spirit who dwell in the cosmos and are intermediaries between higher beings and humankind. They have never walked upon the Earth, and are entities of light who are always around us.

ANGELIC PRESENCE

Angels are androgynous in nature, although they may appear to us in either male or female form. In Genesis 18, for example, Abraham welcomes three angelic guests who at first seem to be travelers. In the next chapter, angels appear again as men, when they visit Job in Sodom. Most of the familiar angels have male names, and archangels (see pages 30–49) have been given male names throughout history. It is not until the Jews are exiled to Babylon that we find descriptions of angels with wings. Some even take on a more frightening appearance, as in the Book of Ezekiel (1:5–13 and 10:10–14).

Many people believe that God created all angels simultaneously on the second day of creation, with the exception of Metatron and Sandalphon (see pages 40–41 and 46)—reputedly the prophets Enoch and Elijah, who then became angels when they ascended to heaven.

SPIRIT GUIDES

Unlike angels, who have never walked upon the Earth, spirit guides once lived on Earth and have chosen to return to help the living. They can be called upon to give advice, comfort, and protection. Many spirit guides work specifically with healers. When I channel my spirit guides to allow them to heal through me, I am aware that different guides come through at different times, depending on who I am treating and why. Some recipients of healing tell me that they sense different sets of hands working on them simultaneously.

I know when my spirit guides are working through me because I feel pulsating waves of heat and often a tingling sensation. I also find that my hands are guided to a particular area of the body that needs attention. My angels, however, use telepathy, which is enhanced especially when I am writing. An angelic presence gives me a warm feeling of excitement.

THE ANGEL HIERARCHY

The word "angel" is both a generic term for a wide range of celestial beings of various "ranks," and a reference to the third level of beings within the third angelic hierarchy, those closest to us here on Earth (see page 15). Angels are divided into hierarchical orders, and opinions differ about the membership of each one. Today, the most widely accepted ranking of angelic beings is that detailed by Pseudo-Dionysius the Areopagite. The surviving writings in Latin, *De ecclesiastica hierarchia* (*On the celestial hierarchy*), thought to have been written some time between 485 and 518–528 CE, describe the now commonly used division into three hierarchies, with each hierarchy containing three orders, or choirs.

First Hierarchy

The angels of the first hierarchy are the closest to God and are of equal rank to each other.

Seraphim (singular: seraph) are the highest order of angels. They are the caretakers of God's throne and encircle it continuously, singing his praises: "Holy, holy, holy is the Lord of Hosts. All the Earth is filled with His glory." It is said that the seraphim radiate an intense blinding light so that nothing, not even the other angelic orders, can look upon them. In Isaiah 6:2, we have a full description of their appearance, with four faces and six wings.

Cherubim (singular: cherub) hold the knowledge of God and are often sent to Earth to perform God's tasks. They are the guardians of light and of the Moon and stars. They are also the record keepers of heaven. Cherubim are the first angels to be mentioned in the Bible, when God sends two to guard the gates to Eden with a flaming sword. In Ezekiel 1:5–8 and 10:21, cherubim are described as having four faces and four wings, with the likeness of human hands under their wings. They do not resemble the cherubs so beloved by painters.

Thrones, or Ofanim are dispensers of God's judgment, acting with impartiality. They are also known as "Wheels" and the "Many-Eyed Ones," as in the Prophet Ezekiel's visions of the Throne of God (Merkavah). In Ezekiel 1, they are described as having the appearance of wheels within wheels, their rims covered with eyes, hence the references to the "Many-Eyed Ones."

Second Hierarchy

The angels of the second hierarchy act as heavenly counselors.

Dominions (Dominations, or Hashmallim) are overseers of the lower angelic realms. They receive their orders from the seraphim, cherubim, or God, and are responsible for keeping the cosmos in order, although they rarely make themselves known to humankind. They wear long gowns and carry emblems of their authority: a golden staff with their right hand and the Seal of God in the left.

Virtues (Fortresses, or Strongholds) lie beyond the thrones and are equal to the principalities (see page 15). They maintain aspects of the material world and are the angels who make miracles occur. People who are able to raise their spiritual consciousness often connect with the virtues. Shaped like sparks of light, they inspire humankind in creative and scientific endeavors.

Powers are angels of birth and death. They guard the boundaries between heaven and Earth, making sure souls leaving the mortal world transcend to heaven safely. They are the keepers of all knowledge of humankind and human experience, known as the Akashic records, and they oversee the distribution of power among humans. They can influence philosophy, theology, religion, and ideology, and they protect the world from the infiltration of demons. They are shaped like brightly colored hazy fumes.

Third Hierarchy

The angels of the third hierarchy act as heavenly messengers.

Principalities are watchers over the mortal world, and are considered to be the guardians of the Earth's nations, cities, towns, and sacred sites. They are concerned with events and issues involving these, including politics and the world's leaders in trade and commerce. They are also charged with managing the duties of the angels, and are thought to be shaped like rays of light.

Archangels are the messengers of God. They act as the administrative leaders of all the angelic orders. Millions of them watch over the entire universe, but specific archangels have been chosen to look after humanity. Archangels work on several different levels, often also belonging to the other choirs or orders, such as cherubim and seraphim.

Angels are watchers over individual souls. There are millions of different types of angels who not only bring joy and love into our lives, but also guide us through every part of our existence on this planet. Angels are mentioned regularly throughout the Old and New Testament, but are not often individually named.

ANGELS ACROSS RELIGIONS

Humankind has always believed in angels. Most of the world's belief systems, including Judaism, Christianity, and Islam embrace celestial beings, the generic term for angels, as part of their cosmologies. Angels play a major role in world religions, and religious texts are fascinating guides to the angelic realms. While most agree that angels are the messengers and servants of God, each religious tradition contributes fresh insights into how angels connect with us.

Zoroastrianism

One of the world's oldest religions, Zoroastrianism originated in what is now Iran. It is based on the teachings of the prophet Zoroaster, also called Zarathushtra or Zartosht (around 1400–1000 BCE). Zoroastrianism recognizes three angelic hierarchies:

- Amesha Spentas (archangels): Literally "beneficent immortals," these are the highest spiritual beings created by Ahura Mazda.
- Fravashis (guardian angels): Each person, through life, is accompanied by a guiding angel. Guardian angels are also known as Arda Fravash (holy guardian angels).
- Yazatas (adorable ones): These spiritual beings are there to help people and to protect them from evil.

Judaism

A number of spiritual beings subordinate to God appear throughout the Old Testament. In some accounts they are indistinguishable from human beings, while in others their appearance varies, such as having multiple faces and wings. Angels appear often but only three are named: Michael, Gabriel, and Satan.

Biblical angels have a variety of roles, including protecting, rescuing, and advising human beings. The Book of Daniel describes Michael as Israel's representative in heaven, and other nations are represented by angelic princes. It also states that there are angelic hierarchies, and that each of us has a guardian angel. Angels also often appear in apocryphal literature—the books written by ancient Jews that were not made part of the Bible, including the Books of the Maccabees and the Books of Enoch (see page 24).

In most Jewish folklore, angels are guardians. Their names are printed on amulets to protect the innocent against demons. An old tradition (Talmud, Shabbat 119b) teaches that two angels (one good, one bad) follow people home on a Shabbat (weekly day of rest). If all is prepared—the challah (traditional bread), wine, and candles—the good angel exclaims, "May it be thus on another Shabbat too," and the evil angel responds unwillingly, "Amen." If all is not prepared, the evil angel exclaims, "May it even be thus on another Shabbat too," and the good angel must respond, "Amen."

Christianity

Angels are prominent in Christian beliefs and appear frequently as the ministers and messengers of God. The Archangel Gabriel, for example, announces the birth of her son St John the Baptist to Elizabeth, and announces to Mary that she will bear the Messiah and that she is to call him Jesus.

Throughout the New Testament it is implied that each individual soul has a guardian or protecting angel, for example:

"Take heed that ye despise not one of these little ones; for I say unto you that in heaven their Angels do always behold the face of my Father, who is in Heaven."

Matthew 18:10, King James Bible

The Catholic Church follows the principal of the hierarchy (or choirs) of angels (see page 12), and the most important are the Archangels Gabriel, Michael, and Raphael. Catholicism views angels as God's instruments of communication, and encourages its devotees to pray for angelic help. Some Protestant theologians, on the other hand, discourage praying to angels.

Islam

Belief in angels is one of the fundamental articles of faith in Islam. The Arabic word for angel is "malak" (plural: mala'ikah), meaning "messenger." Muslims believe that the Angel Jibril (also known as Gabriel) was the messenger through whom Allah (God) revealed the Qur'an (Koran) to the Prophet Muhammad.

Islam teaches that angels are created from light and are invisible. They do not have free will but are completely devoted to serving God, carrying out his commands without question. Angels belong to a level of existence that is beyond the perceptible world, called Alam Al-Ghayb (world of the unseen). They are described as being excessively beautiful in appearance, with different numbers of wings.

Muslims believe that people have two guardian angels: Raqeeb sits on your right shoulder and records all your good deeds while Ateed sits on your left shoulder and records all your bad deeds.

The full number of angels is known only to God, but familiar angels include Jibril (Gabriel), Mikail (Michael), Israfil (Raphael), Azrael, Maalik, Ridwan, Nakir, and Munkar.

Buddhism

Buddhism is also known as Buddha Dharma or Dhamma, which means "teachings of the Awakened One," and was founded around the 5th century BCE by Siddhartha Gautama, commonly known as the Buddha. The Buddhist equivalent of angels are "devas" (celestial beings). In Tibetan Buddhism, devas are sometimes considered to be the emanations of bodhisattvas (enlightened beings). Different schools of Buddhism have various devas who do not normally interfere with human affairs.

The Latter-day Saints

Mormonism is a term used to describe the ideology of the Latter-day Saints movement, which was founded by Joseph Smith in 1830. Mormon was an American prophet (4th century CE) who compiled the records of his people on gold plates. He gave these to his son, Moroni, and they were buried. In the 1820s, Moroni appeared to Smith as an angel, giving him details about the ancient records. Smith retrieved the plates and translated them into the *Book of Mormon*, published in 1830. Mormons believe that people can be baptized after death and that human beings can become gods in the afterlife. Joseph Smith is viewed as a prophet of God.

ANGELS AND KABBALAH

Kabbalah is the mystical aspect of Judaism, an esoteric system of interpreting the Old Testament, Jewish scriptures, and other sacred writings. It is based on the belief that every letter, word, and number contains the mysteries of creation. The word "Kabbalah" comes from the Hebrew "to receive" and refers to a secret oral tradition of teaching. No single book contains all there is to know about Kabbalah, which is intertwined with Jewish folklore. The main Kabbalah texts are the 13th-century *Zohar* (Book of Splendor) and the 2nd-century *Sepher Yetzirah* (Book of Creation or Formation).

According to Kabbalist writings, angels were created before the Earth was made, when God said, "Let there be light." Angels were used in the creation of human beings but then became envious of their free will. There are good and bad angels in the angelic realms; fallen angels (see pages 50–51) are seen as negative messengers, rather than being evil. Some of the main angels mentioned in the Kabbalah are Michael, Gabriel, Uriel, Raphael, and Sandalphon.

The study of Kabbalah can be theoretical (finding hidden meanings in holy texts and writings), meditative (exploring ways of communicating with God through meditation and prayer), and practical (ranging from self-help programs to mystical practices, the main purpose being to help form open channels with the cosmos).

Angels and the tree of life

Kabbalists use the symbol of the tree of life to demonstrate the link between the physical world and the cosmos. The tree is seen as a representation of the universe and of every being living in it, together with their place in the order of things. The basic tree is our immediate terrestrial world, which is overlapped by three more trees, representing the three higher worlds. In order to ascend to our original place in the cosmos from whence we came before birth, we must learn to climb back up the tree spiritually, step by step, layer by layer.

The higher trees are said to be the habitations of angels. Each tree is assigned an archangel to watch over it and to help those who are working spiritually to ascend through it. The highest entities of the angelic world are the holy spirits of the inner council, under the leadership of Metatron, who resides at Kether, the Crown of the Universe. Archangels Michael and Gabriel are the vehicles through which Metatron communicates to Sandalphon at the level of Malkhut. Malkhut represents Kingdom, which is the physical world where humankind exists.

Angels and protection

Kabbalist manuscripts often give instructions for the preparation of amulets with the names of angels inscribed on them. It is usually specified that the amulet must be inscribed by a God-fearing person who has been trained in Kabbalah. Probably among the most well-known amulets are those that protect babies from Lilith. The formula is described in *Sepher Raziel HaMalach*, and refers to Lilith as the first Eve.

THE STORY OF LILITH—THE ANGEL OF THE NIGHT

Portrayed by many as a powerful she-devil, some of us believe that Lilith was, in fact, the world's first feminist. According to some texts, she was Adam's first wife and, like Adam, she was created from the dust of the Earth. Adam expected her to be obedient to his wants and wishes, but Lilith believed that, since they were both created from the same source, they were equal, and she refused to be subservient. Adam tried to force her to obey, so Lilith spoke the magical name of God and left him. Adam prayed to God, asking him to help bring her back. Three angels were dispatched to fetch her but she refused to return. She said that she had been created for the purpose of punishing young infants. The three angels threatened to drown her but let her live after she swore to them in the name of the Lord that if she saw their names, images, or faces upon an amulet in the same room as a baby, she would not touch the child.

THE ANGELS OF ENOCH

The apocryphal Books of Enoch are among the richest sources of angelic lore. Enoch, a prophet who is thought to have lived around 3284–3017 BCE, was the son of Jared, the father of Methuselah, and the great-grandfather of Noah. He is one of two people in the Bible taken up to heaven while still alive:

"And Enoch walked with God: and he was not; for God took him."

Genesis 5:24, King James Bible

He was then appointed guardian of all celestial treasures and chief of the archangels.

Although Enoch is the supposed author of 366 books, which are collectively termed Enochian literature, the most famous of his writings are normally referred to as the First, Second, and Third Books of Enoch.

The first book is considered the most important, and anyone referring to the "Book of Enoch" normally means this one. The only full surviving manuscript is in Ethiopic (an ancient Ethiopian language). The second book details Enoch's journey through the seven heavens (see page 26), predicts the great flood, and contains descriptions of angels residing in heaven. The only known existing manuscript is a Slavonic translation of the original Greek text.

THE FIRST BOOK OF ENOCH

This is divided into different sections:

The Book of Watchers *describes the fall of the angels, the dream vision of Enoch, and his intercession for Azazel and the fallen angels.*

The Book of Parables *discusses the final judgment of Amaze and the watchers and their children, and gives the names and functions of the fallen angels.*

The Book of the Heavenly Luminaires *is concerned with astronomy.*

The Book of Dream Visions *describes the punishment of the fallen angels by the archangels.*

The Book of the Epistle of Enoch *foretells the terrors of the day of judgment and the punishment of sinners.*

The third book is also called the "Hebrew Apocalypse of Enoch" because it survives in Hebrew. The earliest of the three may have been written by different authors some time around the 3rd century BCE. Fragments have been discovered in Qumran among the Dead Sea Scrolls and are thought to have been buried around 70 BCE.

ANGELS AND THE SEVEN HEAVENS

Many see the spiritual universe as made up of seven heavens with the Earth beneath.

1. Vilon/Shamayim/Shamajim: The closest heavenly realm to Earth and governed by the Archangel Gabriel, this is home to the angels who preside over the stars and the elements.
2. Raqia/Rakia: Ruled over by the Archangels Zachariel and Raphael, this is where fallen angels are held prisoner, awaiting the final judgment, and where sinners await the day of judgment.
3. Shechakim/Shehaqim: This is the domain of the Angel Anahel and three subordinate sarim (an order of singing angels). Both paradise and hell are said to be contained within Shechakim.
4. Zevul/Zebhul: Ruled over by the Archangel Michael, it is here that Jerusalem and the Holy Temple exist in the spiritual realm.
5. Ma'on: Governed by the Archangel Sandalphon, here God's praises are sung during the night by choirs of angels.
6. Machon: The realm of Zachiel, this is a stormy, snowy heaven located behind doors of fire. The Akashic records of the Earth's history, and every being who ever lived, are stored here.
7. Aravot/Araboth/Arabot: The highest heaven, under Cassie, houses the throne of glory, attended by the archangels, where God dwells. Underneath the throne lie all unborn human souls.

Angel messages

I call upon the power of the archangels to help light my way to spiritual understanding.

I call upon the archangels because I have begun my spiritual journey and I need help to find my vocation.

I call upon the power of the archangels to surround myself and my family and friends with peace, harmony, understanding, and love.

I call upon the archangels to help me to understand and practice all that they have to teach.

I call upon Gabriel to give me the wisdom that I can be a better person in all my dealings.

I call upon Michael to give me the strength to follow my convictions.

I call upon Uriel to give me insight and clarity in all that I do.

I call upon Metatron to help me to love and approve of myself, and to realize what a special and individual person I am.

I call upon Raphael to help me to seek out knowledge and truth within every situation.

CHAPTER 2

Meet the Angels

All angels, whether archangels, guardian angels, or even fallen angels, fulfill God's purpose. Understanding the virtues of the different archangels will empower you to call upon them for help and guidance for any manner of issue. Recognizing the protective power of your personal guardian angel is an important starting point for opening yourself up to angelic contact.

ARCHANGELS

Archangels can be in many different places simultaneously without restrictions of space and time. They are often the bearers of messages. Although a fundamental part of Jewish, Christian, and Muslim beliefs, archangels are nondenominational, so they will connect with and help anyone, regardless of their beliefs.

References to archangels are found in many different places, including the Bible, the three Books of Enoch, the Qur'an, and the Lists of Dionysius. Among the millions of archangels in the cosmos, only a few are known by name and connect with us on Earth. The names we know all end with "el" apart from Metatron and Sandalphon. These two are considered to be the only archangels

in heaven who were originally mortal. The main Judeo-Christian archangels are often named as Michael, Raphael, Gabriel, Uriel, Chamuel, Jophiel, and Raguel. Traditional Kabbalah (see page 21) adds Metatron, Raziel, Zadkiel, and Sandalphon to this list. Uriel and Ariel appear on some lists as one angel; other sources suggest that they are two different beings. Islam recognizes four archangels—Gabriel (Jibril, Jibrail, Jibraaiy, or Djibril), Michael (Mikail, Mika'il, or Mikaaiyl), Raphael (Israfil or Israafiyl), and Azrael (Izra'il or Ezra'il).

Many people have reached a stage in their spiritual development in which they are communicating, or attempting to communicate, with the archangels.

Ariel

The Archangel Ariel, whose name means "Lion of God," is known as the archangel of the Earth because he watches over the natural world. Together with the Archangel Raphael, Ariel is involved with protecting and healing the environment and wildlife.

Spiritual associations: Ariel will help you to appreciate and have reverence for all life forms, and can help you to understand the realities that surround you.

Azrael

The Archangel Azrael, whose name means "Whom God Helps," is also given the unpleasant title "Angel of Death." Azrael's principal role is to help people cross over to heaven at the time of their physical death. He also surrounds those left grieving on this planet with healing and loving energy.

Azrael is described as having four faces and 4,000 wings, and his body as consisting of eyes and tongues, the number of which corresponds to the number of people on Earth. It is said that every blink of his eyes is a sign that another person has died. He records the births of the living in a large book, and erases the names of those who have died. Azrael is also known as Izra'il or Ezra'il and is one of the four archangels of Islam.

Spiritual associations:

Call upon Azrael for comfort and support in times of grief following a bereavement, for yourself and others.

Gabriel

The Archangel Gabriel, whose name means "God is my strength," may be our most frequent visitor from the higher realms. He is known as the "messenger angel" and is important in Judeo-Christian and Islamic religious lore. In the Old Testament, Gabriel was the angel who destroyed Sodom on the orders of God, and who parted the waters of the Red Sea when the Israelites were fleeing Egypt under the leadership of Moses. In the New Testament, he appeared to both Mary and her cousin Elizabeth to announce the future births of their sons Jesus and John the Baptist. In Islam, Gabriel translates into Jibril, and he revealed the Qur'an to the Prophet Muhammad.

Gabriel is a powerful archangel. Those who need to make an important decision, such as a career change or a house move, should call upon him for wisdom and confidence. He will give you guidance and hope, and help you to focus on your dreams and aspirations. As well as being a direct messenger of the divine, he is charged with looking after the purity of water on Earth and the fertility of all life forms.

Spiritual associations: As well as guiding decisions about your future, Gabriel can assist you in interpreting your dreams, and help you to feel his energies of inspiration, motivation, and wisdom. If you feel that your spiritual vision and energies are blocked, call upon Gabriel to clear your third eye and to remove any other blockages that are hindering you. Also call upon him if you feel your body is full of toxins and needs purifying, or if your thoughts are negative, or even destructive, and they need clearing or cleansing.

Chamuel

The Archangel Chamuel, whose name means "He who sees God" or "He who seeks God," is the archangel of pure love, who can help lift you from the depths of sorrow to find healing in your heart. He is in charge of world peace, and is known by a number of other names, including Camael, Camiel, Camiul, Camniel, Cancel, Jahoel, Kemuel, Khamael, and Seraphiel.

Spiritual associations: Chamuel can help you to build new relationships, both platonic and romantic, on strong and lasting foundations, and he can help to repair misunderstandings. He can teach you to overcome negative feelings toward yourself and others, and he can also help you to express love through creative talents, such as painting and writing. If your heart is broken or bruised, you can call upon Chamuel to help you to mend it. If your heart is blocked through pain or an unforgiving nature, ask Chamuel to help you feel forgiveness.

Haniel

The Archangel Haniel, whose name means the "Grace of God" or the "Glory of God," is generally credited with the title of "Chief or Prince of the Orders of Principalities and Virtues." In some Kabbalist texts, he is known for escorting Enoch to the spiritual realms, where Enoch was transformed into an angel. Haniel can help us to rediscover the lost secrets of natural remedies, such as crystals, herbs, powders, and potions, and to understand how to harness the power of the Moon, and relate to its healing energies. Haniel can be called upon to help those who need poise and confidence before an event, such as speaking in public, being interviewed for a new job, or even going on a first date.

Spiritual associations:

Haniel can help bring inspiration, harmony, common sense, and loving friends into your life. If you feel weak and unsure, call upon the Archangel Haniel to give you strength and determination. He can help you to develop your communication and channeling abilities.

Jeremiel

The Archangel Jeremiel, whose name means "Mercy of God," is the overseer of souls who are waiting to reincarnate. Once we have crossed over, Jeremiel, also known as Ramiel, helps us to look back over our lives on Earth, and while we are still here, he can help us to review our present lives.

Spiritual associations: Archangel Jeremiel will assist you with positive life changes, as well as with the development of your clairvoyant (see page 86) and intuitive abilities in both your waking and dream life. He can help to motivate you if you feel at a crossroads in your spiritual growth and need to find a sense of personal direction.

Jophiel

The Archangel Jophiel, whose name means "Beauty of God," is the patron of artists. He is also known as Iofiel, Iophiel, Jofiel, and Zophiel. He can inspire us to create beautiful images, have positive thoughts, and see the beauty in all things, including people, and he is the archangel through whom all information, perception, knowledge, and ideas flow. Jophiel is involved in helping to cleanse the Earth of pollution and safeguard it against damage, in order to preserve its beauty for the enjoyment of future generations of humankind. See page 131 for a meditation to invoke his help.

Spiritual associations: Jophiel can encourage deeper understanding of yourself and your life's purpose. He can help you to overcome inertia and feelings of depression and low self-esteem, and to discover hidden strengths and abilities within yourself. By helping you to strengthen the connection with your higher self, he can promote your communication with your spiritual guides and angels.

Metatron

The meaning of the Archangel Metatron's name is unclear. Suggestions include "He who occupies the throne next to the Divine throne" and "Angel of the Presence." Many people consider him to be the greatest and most powerful of all the angels. It is said that Metatron once lived upon this Earth in the guise of the prophet and scribe Enoch (see page 24). A scholar of the heavenly secrets, he was taken by God directly to the seventh heaven—the highest level (see page 26). Here, God transformed him into an archangel. In appearance, he is said to have 36 pairs of wings.

Metatron is mentioned in the Kabbalah (see page 21) and is reputed to have been the angel who led the Hebrew tribes through the wilderness to safety after the Exodus. In the New Testament, he is said to have been the light that St Paul encountered on the road to Damascus. He is said to represent divine judgment and to be the overseer of the keepers of the Akashic records, which are thought to be the ethereal memories and thoughts of humankind. He is charged with filtering the pure energy of the cosmos into a vibration that can be used without the destruction of the physical form. He is the patron of children, overseeing their safety and education on Earth as well as helping them to adjust if they cross over to heaven. See page 128 for a meditation to invoke his help.

Spiritual associations: Metatron assists with spiritual growth, encouraging communication with the angelic realms. In sacred geometry, his work is represented by Metatron's Cube, which contains every shape that exists in the universe created by God. Symbolizing the flow of energy through nature, it promotes connection with the peace and harmony of the universe, encouraging us to tune in to our inner self.

Michael

The Archangel Michael was the first angel created by God, and is the leader of the archangels. His name is a question, meaning "Who is like God?" He is one of the greatest of all angels, leading heavenly forces in the fight against the legions of angels of darkness. In the Old Testament, he rescued Daniel and his friends from the lion's den, and in the New Testament he forewarned Mary of her approaching death.

He is often visualized as wearing a cobalt blue cloak and carrying a sword, which is either of metal or a living flame. This sword can cut through cords that bind us to negative emotions and our past, and can protect us from the dark forces that seek to lead us astray. Michael represents courage and strength in mind, body, and spirit. The angel of protection and justice, he is the patron of police officers. See page 134 for a meditation to invoke his help.

Spiritual associations: Call upon Michael to help you banish fear, low self-esteem, and a lack of commitment or motivation. Michael can give you guidance on making changes, and in finding and achieving your life's purpose. Call upon him if you feel afraid for your personal safety. He can protect you from psychic attack.

Raguel

The Archangel Raguel, whose name means "Friend of God," is the champion of underdogs, concerned with fairness, justice, and harmony. He escorted Enoch up to heaven, and is one of the seven archangels listed in the Books of Enoch (see page 24). Raguel keeps all the other archangels and angels in order, making sure that they are working harmoniously with humankind and with each other. His actions have sometimes been misconstrued as being against his fellow angels, leading people to misinterpret his role and consider him a demon. However, he is merely making sure that there is no corruption or wrongdoing. It is said that on the day of judgment he will call forth the other angels to deal with the unpure.

Spiritual associations: Call upon Raguel if you feel you are being manipulated or treated unfairly, or being overpowered by others. He will help you to break free from this pattern, assisting you to find the wisdom and understanding to act with justice when faced with conflict or bullying behavior. Raguel can help you to achieve harmony and balance in your life.

Raphael

The Archangel Raphael, whose name means "God has Healed," is a powerful healer, on both a personal and a planetary level, and is charged with maintaining the atmosphere of the planet. Legend has it that Raphael gave a book of science and knowledge to Noah to rebuild the world after the great flood. Raphael, also known as Labbiel, is said to be the chief of the guardian angels. He is the patron of those who practice in the medical field. Raphael is one of the most frequently depicted angels in western art, painted by Botticelli, Titian, and Rembrandt.

Spiritual associations: Raphael can help with the healing of mind, body, and spirit, assisting with physical and emotional pain. He can encourage you to develop your ability for creative visualization, and enhance your intuitive and clairvoyant capabilities (see page 86). Raphael can even teach you the mysteries of the cosmos.

Raziel

The Archangel Raziel, whose name means "the Secret of God," is believed to know all of the secrets and functions of the universe, and works very closely with God. He is said to have recorded these secrets in The Book of the Angel Raziel, which was given to Adam for guidance after he and Eve were expelled from the Garden of Eden. Raziel also gave a copy to Enoch, prior to his transformation into the Archangel Metatron. The Archangel Raphael is said to have given a copy of this work to Noah, who used the information to build his ark and to help humankind after the great flood. Raziel is the patron of law makers and lawyers.

Spiritual associations: Raziel can help you to comprehend esoteric knowledge, and can assist you in developing your psychic gifts. Raziel can promote your self-awareness and guide you in your search for knowledge, both spiritual and factual, in relation to the physical world.

Sandalphon

The Archangel Sandalphon does not have a traditional meaning for his name, although he is often called "Prince of Prayers." Sandalphon is the Archangel Metatron's twin brother and was formerly the prophet Elijah. As reward for his good work as a mortal man, Elijah was lifted into heaven in a fiery chariot pulled by two fiery horses carried in a whirlwind (Second Book of Kings 2:11). He is said to be the tallest angel, extending from the Earth to heaven. Sandalphon's main role is to carry the prayers of humankind to God, and he also protects unborn children. Guardian of the Earth, he is responsible for the well-being of its inhabitants.

Spiritual associations:

Sandalphon can help you to understand and use the spiritual gifts of healing and distant healing, while making sure that you are "grounded" and thereby protecting you.

Tzaphkiel

The Archangel Tzaphkiel, whose name means "The Scribe of the Divine," is charged with bringing divine laws into physical manifestation and expression. For those who are deserving, he will reveal answers to all their questions and allow them to glimpse the knowledge contained in the Akashic records. Tzaphkiel is often called upon to bring an unwanted situation to an end, or to bring a swift closure to long-term pain. He is closely associated with death and is often perceived as the archangel of death. However, he is also the archangel of life, because without an ending, there cannot be a new beginning, giving the opportunity for transformation.

Spiritual associations: Tzaphkiel can help you to gain wisdom and understanding, and to reach a higher altered state of consciousness by enhancing and accelerating your meditative abilities. This will lead to spiritual progress, increasing your connection with the angelic realms.

Uriel

The Archangel Uriel, whose name means "Fire of God," is concerned with enlightenment, insight, and physical order. He is said to be one of the wisest of the archangels, and is the guardian angel of writers. Uriel is associated with spiritual understanding and studies, and works very closely with the Earth and Earth healing. He is in charge of the weather and with helping the planet to recover from natural disasters, such as earthquakes, hurricanes, tornadoes, and fires. It is said that God sent Uriel to forewarn Noah of the great flood, and that Uriel gave Adam a book of medicinal herbs, and humankind the knowledge of alchemy, Kabbalah, and prophetic visions.

Spiritual associations: Call upon Uriel if you have a problem to solve. You may not realize that he has answered your prayer or question until you suddenly come up with an unexpected solution. Uriel can bring spirituality into your everyday life, while helping you make your way in the material world. He will help you to achieve the goals you set yourself. Uriel will also give you the clarity and insight to understand the hidden agendas of others.

Zadkiel

The Archangel Zadkiel, whose name means "Righteousness of God," is the angel of mercy and compassion and also one of the angels of charity. He is said to be the chief of the order of dominions and one of the seven archangels who stand before the throne of God.

Spiritual associations: Call upon Zadkiel for comfort when you are going through times of despair and sorrow. He can help you to clear your mind of emotional debris, and aspire to higher levels of consciousness, especially when meditating. He can help you to feel kindness and forgiveness toward yourself and others, and to view others with compassion instead of judgment.

FALLEN ANGELS

When we think of dark forces that encourage us to do wrong, names such as the Devil, Satan, Lucifer, Beelzebub, Mephistopheles, and Samael might spring to mind. These are all fallen angels, banished from heaven for disobeying or rebelling against God. The war of attrition of good versus evil, which has been played out since the beginning of time, is, I believe, the so-called devil acting as an agent of God, sent to test the will of man.

The reason why evil exists is to give humanity free choice and duality. Without the presence of evil, humankind would always be in a state of purity and goodness, and therefore there would be no virtue in the good that we do. So those often referred to as "fallen angels" are merely serving the will of the creator by constantly testing the darker side of human nature.

In fact, we are all part of an experiment whereby we constantly have choices placed before us, and it is up to us to follow the pathway of righteousness so that when we return to God after our sojourn here on Earth, we are spiritually richer for the experience. In Isaiah 45:7, God states: "I form the light and create darkness. I make peace and create evil." This demonstrates that he is actually in control of the fallen angels and they are part of his higher plans for us.

The archangel Lucifer was chosen to oversee the angelic forces who would tempt us from our path of goodness. In order to complete his task successfully, he and his followers agreed to be cast down to hell from where, with great gusto, they tempt us into evil and wrongdoing. However, once this grand experiment is completed, Lucifer and his minions will be returned to their true place in heaven.

Once we have been born into our earthly bodies, our memory of our prenatal heritage is forgotten and we have complete free will to choose between positive and negative thoughts and deeds. The battle between good and evil within us is being fought daily. You may think that you are immune to evil thoughts, but jealousy, anger, and ruthlessness are all a part of the human condition. It is important to cultivate an awareness of this struggle and to be determined to choose angelic light over darkness.

GUARDIAN ANGELS

We all have a guardian angel who has been assigned to us by God to protect, guide, comfort, and help us. Your guardian angel has been with you from the time of your first incarnation and will be with you as you journey and evolve through each of your lifetimes. You will never walk upon this Earth alone because your guardian angel will always be alongside you.

"For every soul there is a Guardian watching over it."

Qur'an 86:4

The lessons we are put onto this Earth to learn in each lifetime are already decided—many call this our karma. Our guardian angel is in possession of the blueprint of our lives and spiritual destiny. They will be by your side as you are about to descend to Earth for each incarnation, giving you loving support. After your birth, your guardian angel will be present always, gently pushing and guiding you along the paths of your destiny, encouraging you to develop spiritually and mature as a balanced, integrated human being. They will help to ground you and focus your goals while surrounding you with unconditional love. Your guardian angel will prompt your conscience to know the difference between right and wrong in your thoughts and deeds. However, our guardian angels cannot change our ultimate preordained destiny—which is why, tragically, children sometimes die so young. In these cases, most mystical and religious traditions agree that such souls came to Earth for a short time in order to learn a particular lesson.

A POWERFUL VOICE

Your guardian angel is your personal intermediary when you wish to talk to the higher realms, conveying your problems or need for guidance. Even when a request is not direct, the response can be intense, as businessman Terry Medway told me. A powerful voice in his head warned him whenever he was about to make a bad decision. Although this voice often urged him to take action that appeared inappropriate at the time, it always proved absolutely right. Terry was convinced that this invisible helper was his guardian angel, contacting him so powerfully that he had to take notice and follow the path along which he was guided.

A helping hand

Although our angels cannot help unless we make a pointed effort to invite them into our lives and make themselves known, they often try to commune with us or to help us in various ways—including through dreams, visions, and intuitive thoughts. There are times, however, when your guardian angel will connect with you without conscious invitation. This first contact often happens at times of great physical danger or even life-threatening situations. Your guardian angel will help you in a way that seems coincidental, so you may not realize at the time that you have received a helping hand.

I will never forget a time many years ago, when I was in Israel and had taken my two eldest daughters to a museum. When we came out, we needed to find a taxi to take us back to the hotel. All along the front of the museum were lines of buses, so it was impossible to see the road to hail a taxi. As I stepped out from between two buses to find a taxi, I felt a strong energy pull me back. At the same time, a bus whizzed past at top speed—if I had not been pulled back, the bus would have killed me. Although I did not realize it at the time, my guardian angel had pulled me back, saving my life by a matter of seconds.

Free will

We all have the gift of free will, giving us freedom of choice over which pathways to follow in our life. Your guardian angel cannot stop you if you make the wrong decisions or align yourself with the "dark side" of your nature; but your angel will try to prompt your conscience so you know the difference between right and wrong in all you do. When you begin to open up to connection with the angelic realms, usually the first angel who will converse with you is your guardian angel. One of their primary tasks is to help us to understand how to reconnect with our creator through spiritual growth and knowledge. However, our guardian angels can do nothing for us unless we make an effort to ask them for help or guidance. When the answer comes, remember to thank your guardian angel for their assistance.

Life's problems

Your guardian angel can bring you comfort during dark times and help you to see the light at the end of the tunnel. As our life progresses, we go through many changes, mentally and physically. Our guardian angels help us to overcome negative emotions, to embrace change, and transform the ways we think and act.

If you are having problems with another person—maybe a friend, co-worker, or loved one—ask your guardian angel to have a word with their guardian angel. Together, the guardian angels may be able to help solve the problem. Or, you can try to reach out to their guardian angel directly to let them know how you feel. Often the guardian angels of others are willing to listen and will try to help—as long as their own charge is in no danger of being hurt in any way.

As the world often seems to be in turmoil, and many dangers lurk on our own doorsteps, it is important to try to establish a strong link with our guardian angels so that they can protect us from sources of negativity or evil around us. Do this by frequently calling on your guardian angel to stand alongside you; invocations, meditations, and prayers can also help to strengthen this link.

Your guardian angel's name

To communicate more fully with your guardian angel, it is helpful to find out their name. It is a very human trait to give people and things names because this is our natural way to identify our world. Although our angels do not need names, they are happy for you to call them by name. If you feel that you would like to call your angel by a particular name, go ahead—they will not mind what you call them. Some people find they have a strong feeling about their angel's name, and if you feel this way, don't analyze it—go with the first name that comes to you.

If you would like your angel to give you their name, there are a few ways you can ask for it. First, you need to relax. Either go through a meditative exercise (see page 58), or just take some time out. Become aware of your breathing and, when you feel ready, call out to your guardian angel and ask them their name. The first name that pops into your head will be the answer.

Alternatively, take a sheet of paper and write down your request. Before you go to sleep, contemplate your written request, then put the sheet of paper under your pillow. Your angel's name will come to you—either in a dream, or it will be etched on your mind when you wake up.

ASKING FOR THE NAME OF YOUR GUARDIAN ANGEL

1. Settle comfortably and concentrate on your breathing, inhaling deeply and then exhaling. When you are ready, imagine roots growing from the soles of your feet, penetrating deep into the earth below.

2. Feel the energy from the Earth being drawn up through these roots into your feet, legs, and torso, through to your fingers and then up through your throat to the crown of your head and beyond.

3. Now visualize that the energy flowing from you through the crown of your head is a white light, which forms a channel for your guardian angel's easy communication.

4. Invoke your guardian angel and then ask them their name.

5. Ask them to help you focus on the angels who are surrounding you so that you can understand and develop your communication with them.

6. Visualize that you are opening your mind and body like a flower to hear your guardian angel's name. Feel yourself filled with the power to hear and understand.

7. When you are ready, go back to concentrating on your breathing and close down the energy flowing through the crown of your head. Visualize the energy flowing down through your body and the roots in the soles of your feet, back into the Earth.

8. Thank your guardian angel, and the other angels, and open your eyes.

Angel messages

When the time is right, your angels will always make themselves known to you.

Send out angelic love to the world around you and you can make it a better place.

Your angels like to be invited not only to your celebrations but also to help you overcome life's adversities.

Obstacles are purposefully placed along our paths so that our angels can help us from stumbling.

Random acts of human kindness are inspired by angels.

Lighten up and open up—let your angels brighten up your world and make it a happier place for you.

Many people act like angels when they reach out a helping hand to support and guide you during your darkest hours. Make sure that you learn from these experiences so that you are there for others.

CHAPTER 3

Inviting Angels Into Your Life

Your angels are waiting patiently for you, and when the time is right, they will make their presence known and you will have the blissful experience of connecting with them and welcoming them into your life. Angels love to communicate with us, but the circumstances have to be right in order for us to be aware of their presence.

YOUR SPIRITUAL JOURNEY

There comes a time in many of our lives when we want more than just personal gratification, and embark upon a quest for a more profound set of values, and a life that amounts to more than earning a good wage, having possessions, and entertaining ourselves. We begin to look within for fulfillment and a richer understanding of our spirituality.

Many of you may have begun to seek out spiritual leaders and teachers, through reading or attending workshops, or perhaps by going on a pilgrimage to see world-renowned gurus and healers, such as Mother Meera in Germany, Sai Baba in India, or Buddhist lamas. For each and every one of us, our spiritual journey will be unique. People enter your life at certain times, teach you something, and then depart. Remember that everything happens for a reason. When you are ready, you can invite angels to communicate with you as part of your natural spiritual development. However, although angels love to be able to enter our lives, because we have free will it is usually up to us to invite them.

PERSONAL GROWTH

Life is not easy! We have all suffered setbacks, problems, and sometimes the depths of despair. However, we must remember that we are put on this Earth to learn specific lessons as part of our spiritual growth.

The confidence that we show the outside world often masks an inner need for love, security, and self-belief. It is this submerged part of our personality, where we hide the unacknowledged aspects of ourselves, that we must learn to embrace. By learning to understand ourselves, we can grow emotionally, mentally, and spiritually. We need to acknowledge our shortcomings, such as self-pity, anger, and envy, because the balance of our positive and negative attributes makes us the people we are. You do not have to be perfect to be worthy of angelic communication. Our angels love us unconditionally for who and what we are.

The dark night of the soul

Many people embarking on a journey to raise their spiritual consciousness go through what is called the "dark night of the soul." This journey through the "dark night" often occurs after considerable advancement toward higher consciousness; or, like my own experience, it is a way of pushing you in the right direction for your spiritual growth. It is always a turning point in our lives.

What happened to me changed my world, and the way I think and act, forever. I was very lucky that I was born with a spiritual knowledge, which was encouraged by my late father, who also understood and carried out healing, divination, and many other forms of oral Kabbalah practice (see page 21). However, in the 1950s, it was difficult to find other people open to this type of spirituality. I rarely discussed my knowledge, and in many ways felt compelled to hide it from others.

I got married at 22, had three beautiful daughters, and became a full-time housewife until they grew up and I went to college. I loved doing my history degree but I felt a strong urge to work at a spiritual level and I found myself questioning my life's purpose. In the meantime, my husband had become a successful businessman, founding and running a company. I wanted for nothing, but I was not happy. I knew that I was supposed to be doing something else but had no idea what.

My "dark night" arrived suddenly and unexpectedly when the bank called in the company's loan. Not only did the company have to go, but we also lost our home. Although we were granted a reasonable period to remortgage our home, the bank's lawyer got this cut down to a few weeks, so it was impossible to get the paperwork in place. At the same time, my daughter, who has dyslexia, was doing her final exams.

I went through a time of the darkest despair, although I had to be seen to be strong for the sake of those around me. I found a new house, arranged for the packing to be done, and sorted out as much as I could, but I could not sleep. I could feel my heart pounding with worry, and I would become short of breath. I felt totally alone and found it impossible to discuss my feelings with other people—including my own family. On occasions, I even felt suicidal because the pressure from the bank was relentless.

This period was my "dark night of the soul," although I did not know it at the time. The light had gone out of my life and I felt I was going through the motions of living day-to-day in permanent darkness. I felt totally out of sync with everyone around me. After all, how can people living normal lives understand what it is like to be hounded out of your home? Once we had moved and life became a little better, my spiritual levels began to rise and I became aware of the angels surrounding me. I could hear them as they tried to comfort me. They began to guide me on how I could use my spiritual knowledge to help others. They showed me the way to spiritual growth.

Today, I know that my angels and spiritual guides are always there. I merely have to open up my thoughts to create a direct channel with them. I have written several books about spiritual matters and I also give advice and healing on a regular basis.

What my "dark night of the soul" taught me was to see the world around me in a different light. I have more feeling for the pain and hurt of others and know that the knowledge with which I came into this life is a great gift to be shared with others. Going through the "dark night of the soul" enables us to change our attitudes to ourselves and others, and move to a higher level of spiritual transformation.

OPENING UP TO ANGELIC COMMUNICATION

You will know when the time is right for you to communicate with your angels. Many of you may be aware of the existence of your angels already, so it will come as no surprise when they start to communicate with you. Caroline, a gifted medium, clairvoyant (see page 86), and astrologer, tells me that for every 300 people who come to her for psychic counseling, she sees an angel at the shoulder of one or two of them. Whenever she mentions this to her clients, they are never surprised. It is merely a confirmation of what they intuitively know.

In order to channel angels, it is important that you prepare yourself mentally. You need to create an open, direct line between you and your angels. To do this, you must use part of your mind of which you are not physically aware. Think of manually tuning a radio to a new frequency—this is what you are going to do with your mind, raising your frequency to change levels of awareness to tune in to the spiritual, angelic realms. Your aim is to become a clear and open channel, so that the angels can easily communicate with you and, in turn, you can receive their energies. To assist you in this spiritual transformation, I have developed six steps to help you to achieve communication with the angelic dimensions—see page 68.

SIX STEPS TO ANGELIC COMMUNICATION

Step 1: Feel good about yourself

Many people may feel unworthy of communication at this level. Remember, you are one of God's creations and you were put on this Earth to grow and develop personally and spiritually. Look within yourself and appreciate yourself for who and what you are. Beauty comes from within you.

Take some time to contemplate that this is your life, and you must live it how you see fit. As you grow, so you gather knowledge and a greater understanding of yourself and humanity in general. Realize that you have reached a point where you are seeking something more than just satisfaction and happiness on a physical level.

You may feel guilty about something that is in your past or your present, but you can take steps to free yourself from this. Take a look at what you think you are guilty of and write it down, if it helps. Then make a conscious decision to forgive yourself. For some people, self-punishment through misplaced guilt simply becomes a habit. Forgiveness brings empowerment, and once you have accepted your genuine faults you can heal the past and move on with your life.

Remember:

You are a terrific person and a testament to the miracle of creation.

Every moment of your life should be fresh and exciting.

There is spiritual energy within us all; tap into it whenever you need an extra supply of strength and positivity—open yourself up and feel it. Grow and use it.

Affirm:

I release the past and joyously look forward to the present. I have learned from my mistakes, and this knowledge makes me a better person.

I am surrounded by love, and feel secure in its presence.

I release any anger within, and I love and appreciate myself.

Step 2: Intent

Only you will know if you truly feel comfortable with angelic communication. If you are unsure, visualize that you have already achieved communication with the angelic realms and imagine how you would feel. If you are not completely happy with this, delay this step until you are more confident about your feelings.

Remember:

Your intention must not be for purely selfish reasons, such as helping you win money.

You must really want communication, and should feel ready for it.

Affirm:

This is what I really want. I have been waiting a lifetime for this to happen.

I am ready to open up my heart to angelic love.

I am lovingly and joyously ready to converse with my angels.

I am beyond wondering and now I am wanting.

I want my angels to enter my life.

Step 3: Purpose

Make sure that you understand why you want to allow angels into your life. Define your purpose to yourself. Remember that the angels cannot interfere with the blueprint of your life, nor can they save you from any wrongdoing that you have perpetrated.

Your angels are waiting for you to ask for their help, but your intentions must be honorable. They cannot help you if the principal aim of your contact is to save you from the outcome of your own stupidity and desires.

Your experience in this lifetime is all a part of your karma, your spiritual growth. You must learn from your mistakes and grow with them. However, once you have learned the appropriate lessons, you can ask your angels to help ease and diminish the pain that you may be suffering, and guide you toward a better and more fulfilled life.

Remember:

Your communication must come from deep within your heart and your soul.

Your desire must be honorable.

You place your trust in your angels. You are determined to grow and develop spiritually.

Affirm:

I open up my heart for it to be filled with the purity and light of the angelic realms.

I am treading the pathway of my life but I will now tread it softly and carefully, aware of all of its pitfalls.

I will make my decisions fully aware of the purpose of my life.

I place my trust in my angels to fill me with their love, joy, and harmony, and look forward to it with all my heart.

Step 4: Focus

Now you have decided to focus your intention, you will need to work on ways to open yourself up as a spiritual channel through which the angels can contact you. Clear your mind of chaos, otherwise when the messages come they may be distorted. Meditation is one of the most helpful ways to do this, but there are other methods. I like to sit quietly. You may prefer to walk, use an exercise bike, or engage in any other activity that enables you to focus fully on the present.

The main purpose of this step is to work on your commitment to communication. To begin with, you may sense varying forms of energy around you and flowing through your body. It may take a while for you to become truly aware that these are angelic energies. In order for you to be receptive to the presence of angels, your own spiritual vibrational levels have to be raised, like tuning the strings of a new violin. The angels will help you to achieve total harmony with them. When your spiritual vibrational levels have been lifted, the energies will begin to flow with no impediment.

Remember:

Relax—become peaceful and centered.

Become aware of raising your consciousness to new and unexplored levels.

Allow yourself to become an open channel to the spiritual and angelic realms.

Think about your angels frequently, and invite them into your life.

Do not try to apply logic to how you feel. Use your intuition and go with it.

Affirm:

I am a clear and open channel with my angels.

My angels have always listened to me—the time has come for me to hear them.

I have learned how to reach into my soul to experience raised spiritual consciousness.

I am free of congestion and influence. Cosmic energy can flow freely through me.

Step 5: Communication

Now that you have taken the previous four steps, you are ready to have a two-way discourse with your angels. You need to activate your intent by finding the best and easiest way to open yourself up to talking with your angels. I suggest that you use meditation, affirmation cards, or dream questions. Equally, you can just be still and simply ask.

Remember:

Your angels have been waiting a long time for you to reach this level of spiritual development. They are ready and eager to converse with you. Relax. When the time is right, it will happen.

Affirm:

I feel my guardian angel's wings embrace me.

I am surrounded by the joy, love, and harmony of angels.

I will never feel alone again. I know that my angels love me for who I am, not what I am.

I am grateful that this moment has come, and I look forward to my future life.

Step 6: Gratitude

Always remember to thank your angels for answering your call. They have given you their unconditional love and protection, so remember to send them your love and thanks in return. Even if you have not yet sensed or seen your angels, once you open up your heart and acknowledge their presence, you soon will!

Remember:

Thank your angels for always being alongside you and for answering your call.

Thank your angels for their guidance and constant presence.

Thank your angels for giving you their unconditional love.

Affirm:

Thank you for your constant support. I know that through thick and thin you are always with me, never questioning, always loving.

Thank you for allowing me to become aware of your constant presence, support, and love.

Thank you for communicating to me your love and wisdom. I bathe in the sublime energy and light that I feel washing through me as you make your presence known.

Thank you for just being!

GETTING STARTED

In order to connect and work with your angels, try to be in an environment where you are free from emotional and physical stress and can feel relaxed. Define some personal space for yourself. This could be a particular room or even your whole home—whatever space you claim is the area to focus on. Even the most spiritually experienced or naturally gifted people need to be able to work in an area where they feel comfortable and will not be disturbed by everyday things, such as a cellphone, doorbell, or other noise.

Firstly, get rid of any unnecessary clutter, such as old newspapers and magazines, in your chosen space. Items of furniture may be in the way, so move them somewhere else. Once this is done and your area is tidy, make sure it is clean. Having a clean space with no dust will help you breathe easier and is a much healthier environment for the mind, body, and soul.

Now that you have cleaned your home, open the windows daily to let in fresh air and natural light, and to let out stale energy. Sound can break up stagnant energy. Some people use Tibetan bowls or small Tibetan cymbals to get the right resonance; others may use drums or rattles. One of the easiest ways to use sound is simply to clap your hands, especially in the corners where negative energy can lurk.

Smudging

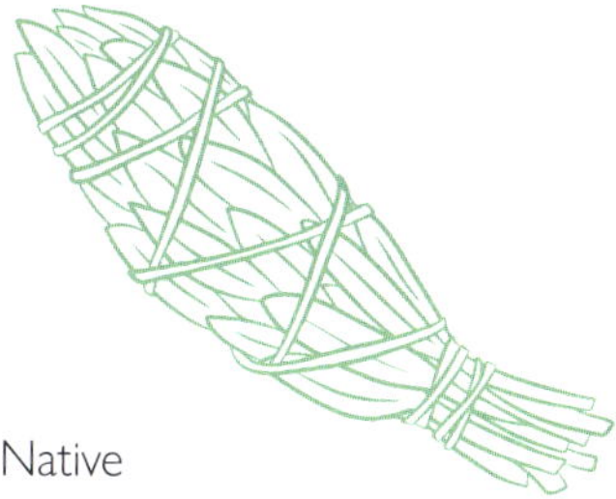

I believe in cleansing my home with smudge sticks on a regular basis. Smudging—a practice that originated in Native American culture—is the burning of herbs or incense for cleansing and purifying. When done correctly, it can bring emotional, physical, and spiritual balance.

The main herbs used in smudge sticks are sage, cedar, juniper, lavender, and sweetgrass—often a mix. Rooms and psychic tools, such as crystals and other objects that hold energy, can be smudged on a regular basis. The main purpose of smudging is to purify and banish any negative vibrations and unwanted energies.

You need to light a smudge stick. I usually hold a small plate under the burning end as I find small parts can fall from it, which can cause damage. The smoke needs to be wafted around the room, especially into the corners. When you have finished, if you have some of the smudge stick left, make sure that it is put out properly—I put it under running water, leave it to dry, and then wrap it up until the next time I want to use it. In our household, when smudging, we also fan the smoke over each family member to clear out any unhealthy energies or vibrations.

MAKING A SACRED SPACE

Many people find it satisfying to make a permanent space in their home where they can find peace and are at ease with themselves. By filling this with articles specifically to help enhance your spiritual vibrations and energy, you are making your own sacred space or angelic altar. Every time you use your special place, some of the energy created when you meditate or concentrate on contacting your angels will linger. This makes it easier each time you return to open yourself up to spiritual and angelic forces. You may find that, as you evolve along this pathway, in time, you will not need to meditate. You may find you have only to enter your sacred space, relax, and think of your intentions to become an open channel to the angelic realms. They will be able to flood you with their energies within seconds or minutes.

Let your angels guide you to the items to place in your space. Remember that the space will affect your mind and senses; it is where you will feel balanced, happy, and secure, and where you will be open to the peace, love, and harmony of your angels. Keep your space clean and warm, and include somewhere comfortable to sit. This could be an armchair, or you may prefer some large pillows on the floor. Remember, though, in most meditations, it is important that the soles of your bare feet touch the floor so that you are "grounded" to the Earth when meditating (see pages 98–99).

Check that your lighting is not too harsh and that you can adjust it to make it right for you. There is nothing better than natural light coming in through a window, but this may not be possible, or you may be able to carry out spiritual work only once it is dark.

Let's explore some other ideas for your space—but remember, the most important thing is that the ambience is exactly right for you.

Music

You may like to play relaxing music when meditating and there are many options for you to choose from. Some people like to listen to classical music, while others prefer New Age music, including Tibetan or Gregorian chants, South American pan pipes, or dolphin songs. Specific compilations of angelic music are available. For others, like myself, music can be a distraction rather than a harmonious helper. I prefer silence when channeling or healing.

Color

A key stimulator for both body and soul, color introduced appropriately into your sacred space will help to raise energy and vibrational levels within. This can be done in a number of ways. The color and fragrance of freshly cut flowers, for instance, offer a wonderful way in which to add natural enhancement to your sacred space.

Candles

Burning candles is particularly helpful to still the mind when meditating. Also, the color of your candles can contribute powerfully to the nature of the contact you need with your angels—see pages 116–117. If you use candles, make sure that you can air your space frequently.

Crystals

These are energy transmitters and I believe it is important to have your favorite crystals around you when working with the angelic and spiritual realms. If you are choosing crystals for the first time, I would suggest clear quartz, which is a powerful energy amplifier, and amethyst, for healing and spirituality, or any crystal that appeals instantly to you—see page 119.

Scent

Burning incense or using aromatherapy oil in a diffuser to work through your sense of smell helps you to relax. Otherwise, you could use fragranced candles, potpourri, or sprays—or even plug-in air fresheners. The part of your brain that detects smell is very closely linked to your emotional center.

AROMATHERAPY OILS FOR RELAXATION

The following aromatherapy oils are readily available and will produce wonderfully calming smells when used in a diffuser: cedarwood, chamomile, geranium, jasmine, lavender, lemongrass, orange, rose, rosemary, rosewood, sage, sandalwood, vanilla.

Angel journal or diary

Most people forget their experiences and feelings in time. Keeping and perusing a journal will help make your connection with your angels stronger and more powerful by focusing your mind, stilling your thoughts, and attracting their love and peace. If you write down your angelic encounters as they happen, you will have a tangible record to keep forever. Dreams should also be written down as soon as possible, because they are easily forgotten. Doing this will give you the opportunity to ask your angels to help you find the hidden meaning of your dreams when meditating.

Personal items

You may want to place photographs of people or places that are meaningful to you in your sacred space, as well as perhaps angel pictures, angel jewelry, crystals, shells, or other items that you have collected on occasions that have happy memories for you. If you do not have the space for a permanent angel altar or sacred space, keep your special items in a pretty box so that it is easy to spread them around you when you are ready to work with them.

A natural sacred space

There is nothing nicer than being able to open up to your angels surrounded by nature. It may take a little time to get used to meditating outside, but persevere—it is worth it! As you get used to channeling your angels while surrounded by the natural world, so you will also become sensitive to using your angel's energies and love for healing on a planetary level.

By creating a sacred space in your own garden, you can incorporate the elements to add more energy. The elements of earth and air will already be present and—if it is a sunny day—fire will also be represented. If you do not have a pond or water feature in your garden, place a bowl of water, the fourth element, near you as you meditate.

You can help to raise the spiritual energy in your garden by growing a variety of herbs and flowers. For herbal inspiration, plant lavender to help you relax, sage for its cleansing properties, rosemary to enhance mental clarity, and mint to help clear your mind and from which to make a refreshing and healthy drink. Choose flowering plants that provide the color with which you wish to surround yourself. Honeysuckle, roses, hyacinth, gardenias, jasmine, and lilac are particularly powerful, both for their color and fragrance, when helping you to connect with your angels.

ANGELIC CONTACT

As the veils between our worlds become thinner, and people seek increasingly to link with the universal consciousness, so it becomes easier to sense angels, but sometimes they appear to us "out of the blue." One of the most common ways they do this is in the guise of human strangers who appear in times of distress as if from nowhere. A lady I met told me this story about two friends of hers who were saved by angelic intervention.

Thomas and Si had rented a holiday home, a farmhouse on the Greek island of Corfu. Located at the end of a deserted clifftop path, the friends decided to hire two mopeds in order to explore the island. Returning to the farmhouse one night after dark, Si's moped lurched from the path toward the steep embankment that led to the cliffside and water below. After frantic searching with no light to guide him, Thomas found Si lying injured.

Although they were miles from the nearest house, a stranger appeared at Thomas's side. He immediately helped Si to his feet. Incredibly, the pain from the injury abated and Si was able to sit astride his moped. As he turned to thank the stranger, he disappeared into the night. The friends were convinced that the stranger was an angel, who had simply appeared when they needed him, before vanishing when his work was done.

There are many instances of angels appearing out of the blue, lending a helping hand and, when we go to thank them, they disappear almost instantly. Often, it is only on their vanishing that we register that we may have experienced the kindness of an angel rather than that of an ordinary good Samaritan.

Angels can throw a powerful shield of protection around you and, if necessary, literally push you out of the way of danger. Some years ago, I remember walking in the West End of London by an office block that was under scaffolding. I was thrown violently away from the building, and off my chosen path, by my invisible guardian angel. Within seconds, a large metal clip that had secured the top part of the scaffolding fell right in front of me. Had I continued walking, I would have been killed or seriously injured.

Feeling your angels connecting with you

Although most people never actually see them, angels can alert you to their existence. Here are some of the tell-tale signs of angelic presence.

Feathers

If a white feather appears from nowhere, some people instinctively know that it is a sign from their angels. If this happens to you, keep your white feather safe to help you connect with your angels.

Synchronicity

Our angels often use coincidence and synchronicity to make us aware of them, or as a nudge to confirm their presence. You may be thinking of your angels in general, or you may be thinking about the name of your guardian angel, when over a short period of time you hear things on the radio or television, or even from friends, that you can link to this. You may even see a billboard with a name that keeps repeating itself. Take these as a sign of the name of your angel.

Flowers

Sometimes you will find that flowers will last longer when placed on an angelic altar or in your sacred space. I have also been told of potted plants that have unexpectedly reflowered when put in these places.

Fragrance

When meditating or thinking of your angels, a beautiful fragrance can suddenly waft unexpectedly through the room.

Sensation

During meditation, when you have invoked your angels, you may feel a tingling sensation around your body or going through your hands like a gentle electric current. If you then ask your angels to show you that this is their energy, you may feel the nature of the tingling change slightly.

Unexpected gifts

If someone, unprompted, thinks to buy you one of the many angelic items available today, take it as a sign that your angels have nudged them toward this purchase.

HOW ANGELS COMMUNICATE WITH US

Angels are God's helpers and messengers. Their connection with us on Earth is a gift from the creator to help us to grow spiritually and eventually understand the very reason for our being. In times gone by, spiritual seekers would spend many years praying, fasting, and meditating in order to be in a position to receive and understand spiritual experiences. Today, as more and more people around the world are becoming increasingly spiritually aware, the whole vibrational energy level of our planet is being raised, making it far easier for our angels to connect with us and vice versa.

The six spiritual senses

You can receive angelic communication, information, love, and guidance through one of your six spiritual senses.

Clairvoyance

The word "clairvoyant" means "clear seeing." Many people are able to communicate with their angels through visual images or a series of pictures that appear in their minds. If you have this gift, dwell upon the image until its meaning becomes clear.

Clairsentience

This means "clear feeling." A clairsentient can sense energies around a person, place, or thing and receive guidance or information through intuition or "gut feeling." The "gut feeling" in question is exactly that—it is centered in your solar plexus, and sometimes feels like you have been punched in the stomach.

Another feeling that you can pick up is of the hairs on the back of your head standing up when you meet someone. My husband has noticed this happen with me a couple of times and has told me that my whole demeanor seems to change when I get very bad "vibes" about someone—which always turns out to be correct! I have worked with this gift since childhood. When I am working on healing with my angels and spiritual guides, waves of energy or heat often come down my arms and through my fingers. They sometimes alternate with a feeling of electrical currents. The person on whom I am working usually feels these sensations in the different areas that are being healed.

Claircognizance

"Clear knowing" is the gift of having spiritual knowledge without knowing how you acquired it. Since childhood, I have realized that I had a special gift. I was born with a spiritual knowledge that is not available to most. I had never read about it—I just simply knew and understood it. From quite a young age I was aware of opening myself up to my angels and spiritual guides and feeling their energy. I considered this to be perfectly normal—I thought that everyone automatically could do healing, use their intuition, understand divination, and translate their dreams.

Clairaudience

"Clear hearing" is the ability to hear in a paranormal manner. This could mean hearing actual sound, or having an impression of sound, similar to the way in which people can think words without them having been audibly spoken. When my angels are channeling their messages to me, this is the way I receive them, and one message after the other comes into my mind. Sometimes, when writing, I may take a break or a "power nap." However, I think my angels take great delight in waking me with more messages so I have to get up quickly in order to write them down before I forget them!

Clairscentist

This means "clear scent." Some people are able to smell fragrances that emanate from the spiritual realms. I have had reports from people who tell me that they can sense when their angel is with them because, from nowhere, they smell a particular fragrance.

Clairgustance

This means "clear tasting." People with this gift are able to taste, or smell, a substance psychically, such as a particular food or drink, without actually putting anything in their mouths.

OTHER WAYS TO HEAR OUR ANGELS

There are many ways in which your angels will try to catch your attention. Here are just a few:

- *Out of nowhere, you hear some beautiful heavenly music—sometimes accompanied by angelic choirs singing.*
- *You hear someone inside your head calling your name.*
- *Angels come constantly to your attention in books and advertisements, and you keep seeing angelic products in shops.*
- *You turn on the radio or television randomly to find a discussion about angels.*
- *You lose something and pray for help, then you look somewhere you would not normally have thought of and the object is there.*

Asking your angels questions

The most natural way to ask questions is to say them in your mind once you feel you are in contact with your angelic helpers. Take a moment and then try to hear or feel the answer. You may wish to invoke your angels by saying something like "Please, my angels, enter my world and help me in my moment of need. I need to know [state your question]." Remember to thank your angels when you have heard an answer.

CALL ON YOUR ANGELS

Another way to ask your angels questions is through meditation.

1. Sit in your sacred space comfortably, remove your shoes, and place your feet flat on the floor.

2. Close your eyes, relax, and concentrate on your breathing. Inhale through your nose for a count of four and exhale through your mouth for a count of four.

3. When you feel completely relaxed, invoke your angels to open a channel of communication with you.

4. Now ask your angels your question, using your heart and mind. Be open to your angels' connection and any feelings, images, or words that you receive. You may wish to write these down so you can contemplate them later.

5. Remember to thank your angels. Focus on your breathing, become aware of your body, and open your eyes.

Some people prefer to write their questions down on a piece of paper, lay it in their sacred space or on their angelic altar, and concentrate on the written word while awaiting the answer. You may wish to write your question down in your angel journal, and also the answer when it comes.

Angels and dreams

One of the easiest ways to contact your angels is to ask them questions through dreams. This method was used by the earliest Kabbalists, and today mystic practitioners often call it "dream incubation." While you are relaxing before sleep, consider your question and then affirm to yourself, either mentally or aloud: "Please, my angels, enter my dreams so that I may learn to hear you. Please help me with [state your request]. I also ask that you help me to remember clearly your message when I awake. Thank you."

If you have a specific question that you would like to ask your angels, meditate on it before you go to sleep. You may also like to write it down so that you can become more focused, and then slip it under your pillow. Do this if your question is very important, and keep a notebook and pen by the bed as you may find that you awake in the middle of the night with the answer, which you should immediately write down before you go back to sleep.

Channeling messages from your angels

Channeling is the way many of us make a direct connection with our angels and the spiritual realms, using our conscious awareness. It is a skill that can be developed by most people with the determination to grow spiritually. When you receive spiritual communication, information, and guidance from your angels, they will commune with you in a language with which you are familiar. This can occur when you are meditating, sleeping, writing, feeling inspired, or relaxing, or even when you are doing creative work. Your angels will usually channel their advice, guidance, and love through one of your spiritual senses (see pages 86–89). To become an open channel with the angelic and spiritual realms, you need first to learn to connect with your inner self. Once you have achieved this, you need to progress to reconnecting with the universe and ultimately with God.

The easiest way to begin this spiritual journey of learning and connection is usually through meditation (see page 98). With time, you may not need to meditate but will find that your angels and guides can come through quickly as soon as you invite them. I have the gift of being an open channel with my angels and spiritual guides. I merely have to ask them to help with healing or to channel their messages for me to write down, and their energies come flowing through. The only disadvantage of this is that sometimes they want my attention when I am busy doing other things. I can be working or out with friends, when suddenly waves of heat or electrical currents flow through me, and I know that I need to get to a quiet place on my own as soon as I can, so that I can receive their messages properly.

Angel messages

You have reached the point in your life when you are ready and willing to reach out and grasp the hands of your angels—they have been waiting a long time for this to happen!

Open up and let your angels and guides into your life.

Feel your angels embrace you and surround you with unconditional love.

Free yourself of your past. Embrace the present and look forward to tomorrow.

The angels will celebrate your triumphs, but will love you as easily for your failings.

Place your trust in your angels and let them guide you through life.

Once you have opened up the lines of communication between yourself and your angels—keep talking.

Your guardian angel will never desert you. Let them fill your life with harmony, peace, and joy.

CHAPTER 4

Working With Angels

There are many ways to work with angels. Meditations, the phases of the Moon, colors, chakras, candles, and crystals are just some of the simple tools you can use to communicate with angels and bring their loving energies into your life.

USING MEDITATIONS

Meditation is the discipline by which we learn to control the mind and so think in an organized manner. In our normal state of mind, we bounce from one thought to another as we receive external sensory stimuli. As a result, we may react in an uncontrolled way, emotionally and/or physically.

We are usually conscious only of our physical existence but, through meditation, we learn to control first our conscious mind, then our subconscious. It is through connecting with the subconscious part of our mind that we begin truly to know ourselves. This is a vital aspect of our journey into spiritual beings.

The main aim of meditation is to reach a higher state of consciousness. This is a difficult state to explain but, put simply, it means we are aiming to use a particular part of our mind that has no conscious access. Most forms of meditation begin with the discipline of breathing control through exercises. Breathing is normally an automatic function that is controlled by our unconscious mind, so, by first concentrating on our breathing, we are expediting a crossover from our conscious to our unconscious mind.

I usually suggest that you sit on a chair so that your feet can rest on the floor—remove your shoes, place your feet flat on the floor, and visualize strong roots growing out of the soles of your feet, anchoring you securely to the Earth. Some of you, however, may prefer to sit cross-legged, or perhaps in the lotus position (legs crossed with each foot placed on the opposite thigh). Another comfortable way to meditate is to lie on your back on the floor. Whichever way comes naturally to you will be the best way so long as you are warm and relaxed.

During meditation, your body temperature can sometimes drop a little, so make sure that you do not get cold. Choose a place where you will not be disturbed. Switch off your cellphone and play some soothing music if you wish. If you are just starting out, it may be a good idea to use a short, guided meditation, so you do not have to think what you need to do next.

It is very important that all meditations are finished properly. Always read the instructions fully and make sure that all the steps for opening yourself up are reversed when closing yourself down.

RAISING CONSCIOUS AWARENESS

This meditation exercise will raise your levels of consciousness and help you learn to ground yourself.

1. Sit on a comfortable chair and place the soles of your bare feet flat on the floor.

2. Concentrate on your breathing. Breathe in through your nose for a count of four and out through your mouth for a count of four. Close your eyes and focus your attention on your body. Beginning with your feet, slowly move your attention up through your legs, thighs, torso, arms, through to your fingertips, neck, and then your head; feel yourself relax throughout.

3. Visualize that you are surrounded by light. As you breathe in, inhale this light and feel it filling your entire body. As you breathe out, exhale all the tension and pain that you feel throughout your body. If your mind begins to wander, bring your attention back to your breathing and focus on it.

4. When you feel ready, visualize that you have strong roots growing from the soles of your feet, pushing their way into the ground below, no matter how many floors up you may be. Visualize them burrowing into the Earth.

5. When you next inhale, visualize the energy of the Earth being sucked up through the roots into your body. With each breath, imagine more and more of the Earth's energy entering you, working its way up through your feet, toes, legs, torso, arms, fingers, neck, and head, until it fills every part of you.

6. Visualize that the crown of your head has an opening and through it rays of energy are reaching up to the sky and out farther into the cosmos. As you inhale, visualize the energy of the cosmos being drawn into your mind, head, and body through these rays and feel it gradually filling every part of you.

7. Now breathe in the two energies together. Inhale both the energy coming up through you from the Earth, while at the same time feel the energy of the cosmos filling your mind and heart. Bathe in these energies for as long as you like. You are now connected to both the universe and the Earth.

8. Ask your angels to enter your life and to fill and surround you with their gifts of love, peace, tranquility, and joy. Sense them connecting with you and bathe in the wonderful feeling it brings. Stay here for as long as you want.

9. When you are ready, thank your angels for their gifts and again focus on your breathing. Feel the energy of the cosmos retreat from your body, back through its linking rays. Feel its connection with your body dissolve and visualize the opening in your crown close. Feel the energy that has filled you from the Earth descend back down from your head, neck, fingers, arms, torso, thighs, legs, through to your feet. Visualize the energy going back down to its place of origin, through the roots that have been anchoring you to the Earth. Visualize the roots that have been growing from the soles of your feet dissolving away.

10. Concentrate on your breathing and become aware of your body and where you are sitting. Become aware of your heartbeat and the sounds around you. Take your time; when you are ready, open your eyes.

USING THE ENERGIES OF THE MOON

The phases of the Moon can greatly influence our lives. Kabbalists and many other spiritual seekers have rarely embarked upon important deeds and actions without first having taken into account the phases of the Moon. The New and Full Moon periods are times of intense spiritual and magical focus. I always like to program my crystals (see page 120) under the light of a Full Moon. It also can be beneficial when working with your angels to link the energy of the Moon with what is going on in your life.

New Moon and Waxing Moon

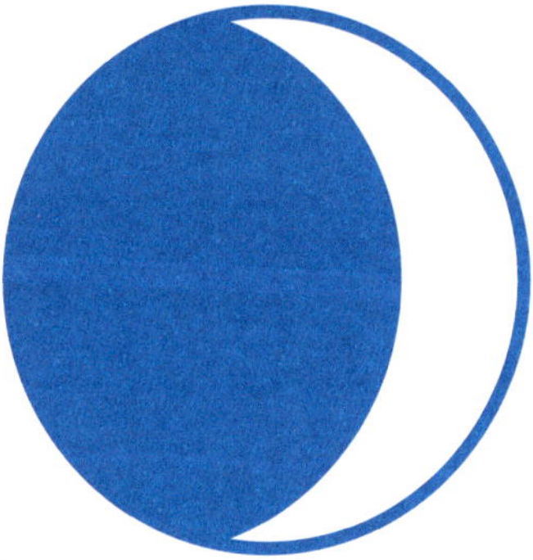

The waxing Moon is the period of about 15 days from the New Moon to the Full Moon, when the Moon is increasing in size. This is the best time for new beginnings, such as starting a new project or a new job, or moving house. It is also a good time to ask for abundance, forgiveness, protection, and wisdom.

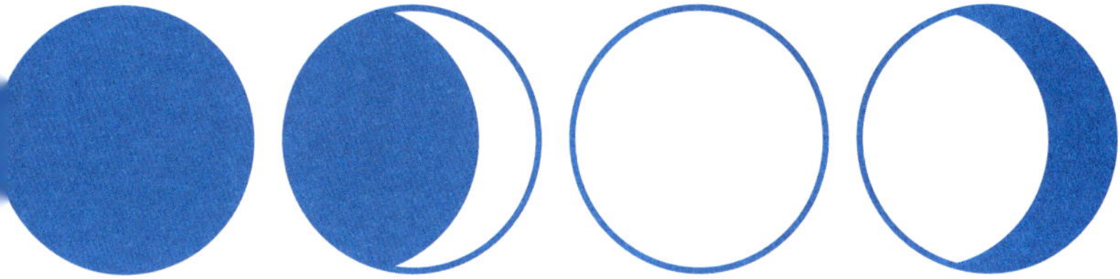

Full Moon

The Moon's power is strongest when it is full. This is the best time, especially for those less experienced in angelic communication, to meditate and let the power of the Moon enhance your spiritual development and energy. During this period, all communication, both physical and spiritual, is strengthened by natural lunar energy. Use it to develop your psychic powers and spiritual knowledge. This is also a good period to forgive yourself and others, use your intuition, be open to communication through dreams, and wish for good things in the future.

Waning Moon

The Moon begins to lose its power as it diminishes in size. This period lasts about 15 days from the date of the Full Moon, and is the time when you should let go of things, break bad habits, move on, and liberate yourself.

ANGELS AND THE RAYS

The seven great rays of creation provide a powerful connection with the archangels (see pages 30–49). A ray is a force, or energy, and when we begin to access the vibration of each ray, changes can occur in our lives. Working with the rays can open us up to new levels of spirituality, allowing us to progress beyond the confines of our five Earth-bound physical senses to those of clairaudience (see page 88), intuition, telepathy, clairvoyance (see page 86), and connection with the cosmos. Each ray manifests its own color in the physical world, but each also has a color on the spiritual plane, for those who can see it, so they sometimes appear differently.

ANGELS AND COLOR

Most of us use a form of color therapy in our everyday lives without even realizing it. Every color has its own vibration and energy, which can affect us subconsciously even if we are unaware of it at a conscious level. Once you become aware of this, you may realize that your interaction with the world around you differs when you wear clothing or jewelry in particular colors. We are attracted to those colors because we need to bring their energies into our lives. As we progress spiritually, we become aware of how color can provide a sense of wholeness and well-being. By using color, our channels of communication with our angels can be accelerated and greatly enhanced.

Being able to use the rays is a key element in our spiritual evolution. Rays can help contribute to knowledge about ourselves and our part in the cosmos. Each one has its own archangel, who connects with it on a vibrational level. You can call upon these "Archangels of the Rays" through meditation (see page 109). When you do so, a fragrance may suddenly permeate the air around you, since certain fragrances carry the same vibrational levels as the rays. If you wish to communicate specifically with one Archangel of the Rays, you could use candles of the related color to help focus your mind.

RAY 1 THE BLUE RAY

Archangel Michael's Ray of Protection and Power

Other Main Properties
Love, Faith, Motivation, Strength, Calm, Transformation, Harmony, Courage

Associated Crystals
Blue Kunzite, Blue Topaz, Lapis Lazuli

Associated Fragrances
Cedar, Frankincense, Geranium, Myrrh, Palmarosa, Sage, Tea Tree

The strength of a powerful warrior is combined with a love and tenderness that can fill your entire being. Connection with this ray can help you to heal and purify your physical body, allowing you to develop your feelings of humility, peace, love, serenity, and spirituality, thus changing your outlook and attitude to the world around you.

RAY 2 THE YELLOW RAY

Archangel Jophiel's Ray of Illumination and Wisdom

Other Main Properties
Optimism, Joy, Fun, Knowledge

Associated Crystals
Amber, Citrine, Yellow Sapphire, Yellow Topaz

Associated Fragrances
Cinnamon, Clove, Pine, Sandalwood

The gifts of love, light, and warmth may permeate every cell of your being, helping you to connect with your soul, which in turn will strengthen your communication with your spiritual guides and your angels. Through utilizing the strength of this ray, you can learn to appreciate the beauty within others and to cherish the wonders of life.

RAY 3 THE PINK RAY

Archangel Chamuel's Ray of Love and Relationships

Other Main Properties
Hope, Intuition, Gratitude, Tolerance, Compassion

Associated Crystals
Pink Kunzite, Pink Tourmaline, Rose Quartz, and the metal Silver

Associated Fragrances
Jasmine, Gardenia, Hyacinth, Rose Otto, Ylang-Ylang

Gentle, flowing energy brings warmth to your heart, body, and soul. It will open up your heart to develop healing gifts and attract to you like-minded soulmates. It can help to repair strained friendships and enhance your relationships. The focus of this ray will help you to appreciate life and the world around you, encouraging you to value your "uniqueness" and to develop and use your talents.

RAY 4 THE WHITE RAY

Archangel Gabriel's Ray of Harmony and Purity

Other Main Properties
Understanding, Clarity, Creativeness, Grace, Purity

Associated Crystals
Clear White Quartz, Diamond, White Sapphire

Associated Fragrances
Basil, Bay, Clary Sage, Nag Champa, Neroli, Rose

The loving, powerful energy of the White Ray contains and reflects all colors, merging them to form a brilliant white that will help bring accelerated and unprecedented spiritual growth and enlightenment. This ray will help you to realize and understand your true potential and to accomplish what is necessary in order to achieve your goals in life.

RAY 5 THE GREEN RAY

Archangel Raphael's Ray of Healing

Other Main Properties
Humility, Flawlessness, Communication, Intellect, Adaptability

Associated Crystals
Emerald, Green Peridot, Green Tourmaline, Moldavite

Associated Fragrances
Mint, Pine, Sage, Wintergreen

This ray combines green, the color of nature, with the radiant power of the Sun to create vitality, truth, beauty, and healing. It will invite harmony into your life and help keep physical, mental, and emotional energy balanced. It will enhance creative visualization, divine visions, and intuition, enabling you to focus and seek the truth in all that you do.

RAY 6 THE GOLD RAY

Archangel Uriel's Ray of Compassion and Peace

Other Main Properties
Serenity, Honesty, Confidence, Courage, Justice

Associated Crystals
Rutile Quartz and the metals Yellow and White Gold

Associated Fragrances
Cinnamon, Chamomile, Ginger, Neroli

Peaceful, graceful, and full of love, this ray can fill every part of your being with its energy. Its main focus is to encourage the development and use of spiritual knowledge and energy in order to serve both God and man. Many see flecks of other colors in it—normally ruby and/or deep purple—giving rise to its alternative names, Ruby Ray or Ruby-Gold Ray.

RAY 7 THE VIOLET RAY

Archangel Zadkiel's Ray of Purification and Spiritual Growth

Other Main Properties
Joy, Calm, Mercy, Forgiveness, Transformation, Grace

Associated Crystal
Amethyst

Associated Fragrances
Lavender, Lilac

Calming energy combines with the love of the universe, entering your heart and the very essence of your being—your soul. The energy of this ray not only focuses on forgiveness, purification, and grace, but its powerful vibrations will help you learn how to open yourself up to become a channel with the angelic realms.

CONNECTING WITH THE ARCHANGELS OF THE RAYS

1. Settle in a quiet place or your sacred space (see page 76), concentrate on your breathing, and ground yourself by visualizing strong roots growing from the soles of your feet. As you inhale, feel the energies of the Earth draw up into you until they fill your whole body.

2. Invoke Archangel Michael to fill both your physical body and your aura (the energy field that surrounds it) with his Blue Ray of Protection. Visualize his ray entering the crown of your head and spreading around your whole body, expanding to fill your aura. Ask him to fill you with strength and courage. Ask him to draw his sword and cut any cords and attachments binding you to negative thoughts or deeds. Be open to his energy and his words. When you feel this process is complete, thank him.

3. Now invoke the Archangel Jophiel to pour the Yellow Ray through the crown of your head to fill your mind with the knowledge and wisdom that you have learned since childhood. Ask him to help you so you can teach and help others. Be open to his energy. Thank him and move on.

4. Now open your heart to the Pink Ray of the Archangel Chamuel and visualize it penetrating your physical body as it enters your heart. Invoke him to help you find love, compassion, and the strength to forgive those who may have hurt you. Ask him also to forgive you for any hurt you may have caused others. Thank him and move on.

5. Now feel the Archangel Gabriel pour the White Ray of Harmony and Purity through the crown of your head, filling your physical self and your aura. Ask for clarity in understanding the lessons you should be learning and to help you clear any blockages holding you back. Ask him to fill your life with joy and generosity to others. Wait for the Archangel Gabriel to do his work and thank him.

6. Next is the Green Ray of the Archangel Raphael. Visualize him pouring his Ray of Healing into your physical body, through the crown of your head. If you are ill, ask him to help you; if you know others who are ill, ask him to send his Green Ray to help them. Be open to any communication from the Archangel Raphael, then thank him and move on.

7. Now invoke the Archangel Uriel to fill your aura and mind with his Gold Ray of Compassion and Peace. Ask him to help you send out a feeling of serenity to others you know, and those who may be going through difficulties. When you have done this, pause so the Archangel Uriel can complete his work. Be open to his energies and his words. Thank him.

8. The last is the Violet Ray of the Archangel Zadkiel. Visualize him pouring this ray through your crown so that it spreads through your physical body and fills your aura. Ask the Archangel Zadkiel to dissolve your feelings of negativity and replace them with joy and happiness. Allow the Archangel Zadkiel to do his work, then be open to any communication he may have for you. Thank him.

9. You are now filled with the power and energy of these seven archangels. Take time to enjoy their love and feel their healing energy.

10. When you are ready, you will need to close down your spiritual centers of heavenly communication. Concentrate on your breathing and feel any spiritual energy left within you rise up through the crown of your head. Visualize it flowing back to the cosmos, then visualize the top of your head closing the portal through which the energy entered your body. Visualize the energy of the Earth melting out of your entire being slowly. Take your time, open your eyes, and become aware of your physical body. Notice how renewed you feel.

THE CHAKRAS

Our knowledge of the chakra system comes from the study of ancient Indian texts. In Sanskrit, "chakra" means "wheel" and those who can see them describe the chakra points as spinning wheels of light.

There are seven major chakra points used in meditation, which are all interrelated. If one chakra point becomes disturbed or blocked, it can upset the functioning of the others—this can manifest itself as an emotional feeling of being depressed, with negativity blocking spiritual attunement and growth. If this blockage remains in place, physical problems can develop, stemming from whichever area is most vulnerable. Specific archangels are in charge of helping the development of each chakra.

Each chakra has a different function and vibrates at a different frequency. The vibration of the color associated with each chakra is an important ingredient in connecting your physical body with the cosmos. When working with the chakras to help your spiritual development, using crystals can enhance your connection—the vibrational energy of the crystal's color working with the colors of the chakras adds extra power. The best way to work with crystals is to lie on the floor and lay the specific crystal on the chakra point. See pages 118–120 to find out more about working with crystals.

First or Base Chakra

Archangel Gabriel

Location Base of spine
Function Grounding
Associated color Red
Associated crystals Red Jasper, Red Tiger's Eye
Related physical areas Large intestine, adrenal system, rectum, muscles, lower back, legs, and feet

Second or Sacral Chakra

Archangel Gabriel

Location Lower abdomen just above the pelvic bone
Function Sexuality and creativity
Associated color Orange
Associated crystal Carnelian
Related physical areas and illness Lower intestine, kidneys, reproductive organs, hormones, bladder, bowels, bronchitis, asthma, blood circulatory system

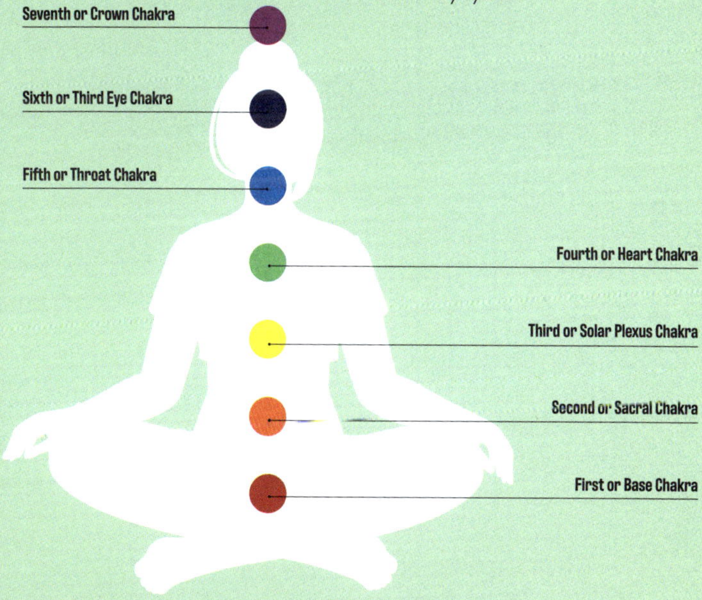

Third or Solar Plexus Chakra

Archangel Jophiel

Location Navel and solar plexus area
Function Personal power and self-confidence
Associated color Yellow
Associated crystals Citrine, Amber, Yellow Tiger's Eye
Related physical areas Digestive system, liver, gall bladder, spleen

Fourth or Heart Chakra

Archangel Raphael

Location Heart
Function Love, healing, and emotional well-being
Associated color Green
Associated crystals Emerald, Peridot, Aventurine, Amazonite, Malachite
Related physical areas and illness Heart conditions, thymus gland, immune system, headaches, migraine, and related symptoms of stress

Fifth or Throat Chakra

Archangel Michael

Location Throat
Function Communication and mental creativity
Associated color Blue
Associated crystals Sodalite, Blue Howlite
Related physical areas and illness Thyroid system, weight and its associated problems, teeth and gums

Sixth or Third Eye Chakra

Archangel Raziel

Location Between the eyebrows
Function Inner wisdom and intuition
Associated color Indigo
Associated crystal Lapis Lazuli
Related physical areas and illness Head, eyes, ears, nose, pituitary gland, and headaches

Seventh or Crown Chakra

Archangel Zadkiel

Location Crown of the head
Function Spiritual understanding
Associated color Violet
Associated crystal Amethyst
Related physical areas and illness Immune system, pain relief, and the physical healing process

ANGELS AND CANDLES

Colored candles are a tool to help you focus your mind and raise your vibrational levels, so that you can become an open channel with the cosmos. Colors have different associations, or meanings, assigned to them, and you can choose to work with a particular candle color that matches with your intention—see pages 116–117.

Preparing and using candles

Go to a quiet place, your sacred space, or your angelic altar (see page 76). Before you begin, you may wish to dedicate your candle specifically to your angelic communication. Hold your candle in both hands, still your mind, and concentrate as you ask a particular archangel, or your angels in general, to come through for you, using words that feel right.

An example of what you might say is: "I dedicate this [state color] candle to you and invite you to come into my life. Let your love and harmony surround me. I open up my heart and soul to you and welcome you." Become peaceful and centered and allow yourself to become an open channel.

When burning a candle for this purpose, you may wish to let it burn through until it is finished—in which case it is very important not to leave the candle unattended as it could be a fire hazard. Alternatively, you may prefer to blow the candle out once you have finished your meditations, as this can help to give a feeling of closure. If you are using your candle for only a short period, you may wish to use it again later for the same purpose. Once the candle has cooled down, either leave it in its holder—as long as no one will touch it—or wrap it up to keep it protected until you want to use it again.

PURPOSE OF SPECIFIC COLORS

It may help you to focus your mind on specific intentions if you light the candle of the relevant color. Remember that white can replace all other colors.

White: *Spirituality, peace, tranquility, harmony, clairvoyance, meditation, inner peace, and truth.*

Red: *Energy, strength, courage, vitality, and willpower. Can stimulate sexual passion, lust, and virility.*

Pink: *Love, both romantic and platonic. Encourages affection, friendship, romance, success, kindness, gentleness, and willpower.*

Purple: *Psychic and spiritual abilities, spiritual growth, power, ambition, material wealth, wisdom, and healing.*

Black: *Protection—helps remove negative energy by absorbing it. If you are alone, can help you to feel safe.*

Silver: *Clairvoyance, inspiration, intuition, dreams, higher wisdom, intellect, purity, compassion, and inner stability.*

Gold: *Positive influences and happiness, confidence, understanding, memory, concentration, creativity, imagination, and knowledge.*

Yellow: *Confidence, intellect, memory, visualization, happiness, vitality, attraction, and charm.*

Green: *Spiritual healing, luck, good fortune, money, and prosperity—although remember that financial gain must not lead to greed.*

Orange: *Courage, study, intellect, knowledge, creativity, and understanding. Good for career, business/monetary matters and for helping to bring legal matters to a conclusion.*

Blue: *Higher wisdom, inner peace, inspiration, intuition, dreams, truth, and understanding.*

Never leave burning candles unattended.

WORKING WITH CRYSTALS

Crystals have been treasured for both their beauty and their energy since the dawn of civilization. They are part of the heritage of humankind, having been formed within the bowels of Mother Earth, never losing their color and brilliance. Priests, shamans, spiritual seekers, and healers have used them for thousands of years.

Each crystal exhibits its own individual pulse of energy. This energy can help us enhance and amplify the strength of the communications our angels are sending us, very much like using a megaphone. The energies found within the world of minerals are a gift from the cosmos, so when you access and use these energies, you are connecting with a tool that has been made available to help us connect with the universe.

Crystals have physical form and structure that link us to the physical world around us, but they also have particular energies that can help our spiritual journey. Every crystalline structure is unique, with its own color, form, and energy. Each can be used in a distinctive way, not only to understand the nature of our existence on this planet, but also to help us explore the heavenly realms.

Choosing your crystals

There are a number of ways to choose crystals. You can look at a list of their properties, and decide which ones to buy from that. Some people prefer to dowse for their crystal with a pendulum, or simply pass their hand over a selection to see if they can feel a slight vibration. Another way is to look at a selection of crystals and just go with your gut feeling, choosing the one that appeals to you most. There is a saying that you do not choose the crystal—it chooses you. When buying crystals, keep in mind that some may have been dyed, and it is always better to try to buy natural crystal.

Cleansing and programming your crystals

It is important to cleanse your crystals properly because crystals retain the memory of everyone who has touched them, so you need to wipe this memory clean. Ideally, they should be washed in the sea or natural running water, but if this is not possible, I suggest soaking them in water containing sea salt or washing them under a running faucet instead—but bear in mind that a number of fragile crystals, such as moldavite, should not be put in salt water. Some people bury their crystals in their garden to cleanse them—if you do this, make sure you mark the place so that you can find them again! Another way to cleanse them is to use a smudge stick, allowing its smoke to surround the crystals—see page 75.

Once your crystals are cleansed, you must program them. This is to tell their energies how you want to use them—perhaps for attunement or transformation. The most practical way to do this is to hold the crystal in your hand and affirm inwardly the purpose for which it will be used, whether for healing, love, or meditation. Alternatively, you can devise a precise affirmation that will accurately describe the purpose of the programming—for instance, to be an open channel with the angelic realms. Do not let others touch your crystals once they have been cleansed and programmed, because the crystals will pick up and store their vibrations and energies.

Using crystals

Hold your crystal in your non-dominant hand. With practice, you will be able to feel the subtle electric currents contained within the crystal. There are a number of ways in which to work with your crystals—the best thing, as always, is to go with the flow and work however you feel most comfortable. If you are drawn intuitively to particular crystals, those will be the best ones for you to use.

Angel messages

Some doors may close to me, but I know that others will always be open.

When I invite my angels to gather around me, I know that the whole of humankind will benefit.

Not a day passes when I do not feel the love, happiness, and compassion of my angels.

The presence of my angels has blessed my life in ways that I could never have foreseen.

I invite my angels to help me to let go of the past so that I can have peace in the present.

I place my trust in my angels to help me to make the best of this life.

My angels fill me with the energy and light of the universe.

CHAPTER 5

Our Guides Through Life

We must trust that our angels will always help us through any kind of adversity that we may encounter. You can call upon your angels to assist with all kinds of problems—large or small. With loving patience and care, they will gently guide us through to the next stage of our lives.

ANGELIC WISDOM

As a result of angelic guidance, we can look beyond difficulties so that we can move on. By asking our angels for help and inviting them into our lives, we not only open ourselves up to their energies—which will surround and feed us with love, hope, happiness, and tolerance—but we benefit the whole of humankind.

There will be many times throughout your life that you will feel in need of the care and loving guidance of angels. Love, marriage, and having children are all wonderful, joyous life experiences but they rarely, if ever, come without struggle and adversity. Death, particularly of a loved one, is a time when we can benefit the most from the help of angels.

HOW TO ASK YOUR ANGELS FOR HELP

On a day-to-day basis, your angels will try to guide and assist you if and when you ask for help. Follow the meditation below, ensuring that you are fully relaxed before making your request to your angels.

1. Go to a quiet place or your sacred space (see page 76) where you will not be disturbed. Settle comfortably and concentrate on your breathing until you feel really relaxed.

2. Sense within yourself that you would like to be an open channel with the angelic realms by inviting in your angelic helpers.

3. Feel their energy begin to surround you, and then permeate through your body.

4. When you feel ready, ask them for help with your problems. Be aware of your cry for help coming from the depth of your very being.

5. Concentrate on your request.

6. When you feel ready to move on, concentrate on your breathing again as you feel the angelic energies dissolve from your environment.

ANGELS AND CHILDREN

When we are born, our prenatal knowledge is mainly forgotten, but children often retain a small iota of memory of their previous existence in the spiritual world, and some memory of their past lifetimes in the physical world. Often children play with "invisible friends." They may be invisible to us but they are very real to young children who have not yet totally broken their ties with their spiritual origins, and who are still able to see the spiritual realms.

This is what happened with my youngest daughter, Alexis. We moved house six weeks after Alexis's birth. We had bought the house from the children of the woman who had actually had it built in 1934, and the house was sold to us just after her death. We were told how she had loved to sit in the living room and look onto the golf course behind the garden. When Alexis was small, I would often see her waving from the garden toward the house. When I asked her who she was waving to, she said that an old lady was watching us, and that she was happy that her garden was still being enjoyed. Alexis said she often saw this lady.

A child's memories of the prenatal spiritual worlds are thought to diminish over time, due to the strong vibrations from our planet that surround children, the energies from our earthly homes, and children's need to belong to their peer group. By this, I mean that once children go into full-time education, their natural, spiritual intuition can close down. However, within many children, a small, distant memory lingers about their guardian and birthing angels, and they are able to reproduce wonderful drawings and paintings of angels, even though they cannot remember actually ever seeing a picture of one.

It is human nature to worry about your children, but worry is a dark, negative force, which can unintentionally affect those at whom it is directed. Our children are psychically linked to us and we should remain consciously aware of sending positive, loving, protective thoughts to them. Open up to their guardian angels and ask them to surround your children with rays of protection and love. By doing this, you will bring your children's guardian angels that little bit closer to them. You could also reach out to the Archangel Metatron, the patron of children, through meditation and ask him to watch over your children (see page 128).

PROTECT YOUR CHILDREN

The Archangel Metatron (see page 40) is the patron of children, and you could invoke his help to protect your children.

1. Find a quiet place where you will not be disturbed; sit down, relax, and close your eyes.

2. Concentrate on your breathing and, when you feel ready, call upon the Archangel Metatron to help you.

3. Invoke him to send his protecting and loving energies to your child or children. Visualize them as you do this, and see them in your mind's eye surrounded by a soft cloud, like a soap bubble, of whichever color you want.

4. Ask the Archangel Metatron to watch over them and keep them safe. You can also ask him to help them gain wisdom and knowledge.

5. Take your time and remember to thank the Archangel Metatron when he is finished. When you feel ready, open your eyes.

ANGELS, PARTNERSHIP, AND MARRIAGE

The marriage or partnership ceremony of two people who are truly in love is a wonderful occasion; realms of angels attend, wishing love and joy upon the couple. Heavenly choirs sing in celebration of two soulmates having found each other and vowing to entwine their lives together. When people are in love, their vibrational level shifts, naturally opening them up to letting their angels work closely with them. This is why when people are in love, their whole demeanor appears to change. They seem to be filled with happiness and exhilaration, and will see their partner in the best light.

However, if the relationship starts to take a turn for the worse, you will notice that the atmosphere gets heavier as the natural open channel of communication with the angels begins to close down. The Archangel Chamuel (see page 36) is in charge of love and relationships, and it is he from whom you should request help if you have problems in this area. Call upon him if you want to find a new loving relationship, either romantic or platonic, or new like-minded friends. Once these are found, the Archangel Chamuel will help you to build and sustain your relationships.

EVERYDAY ANGELS

If invited, angels can play an important part in our everyday lives. These are angels who have special skills relevant to all aspects of our lives, and they can offer help to ourselves and others.

Education and creativity

The Archangel Jophiel (see page 39) is also known as the Angel of Illumination. All ideas, perception, and knowledge stem from him, and he can help us to discover abilities we did not know we possessed. He can inspire our thirst for knowledge and creativity, while simultaneously encouraging our development for the highest good. For overcoming feelings of depression and low self-esteem, his help is invaluable. He works with the Yellow Ray of Illumination and Wisdom (see page 106).

GAIN UNDERSTANDING AND INSIGHT

This short exercise can help you connect with the Archangel Jophiel.

1. Go to a quiet place, sit comfortably, relax, and concentrate on your breathing.

2. When you feel fully relaxed, visualize as you inhale that you are breathing in the Yellow Ray of the Archangel Jophiel (see page 106). Visualize it filling every part of you.

3. Now invoke the Archangel Jophiel to connect with you, asking him to grant you the gifts of wisdom, understanding, and creativity. Feel his energy beside you. If you need help with a problem or feel low, ask him to help you. If you feel that your creative juices are blocked, ask him to clear them.

4. When you are finished, remember to thank the Archangel Jophiel and be attentive to any message he may have for you. Be aware of him leaving your side and the Yellow Ray leaving your body slowly at the same time as you exhale your breath.

5. When you are ready, open your eyes.

Wisdom and self-esteem

We all have insecurities that every now and then nag away at us. Many of these probably began years ago, when perhaps our parents, teachers, or partners made us feel that we had done something wrong, or perhaps we were made to feel that our achievements were never good enough. If we dwell on negative thoughts, it can hold us back from achieving the good things in life. In extreme cases, it may also lead to physical illness. The Angel Zagzagel is the angel of wisdom, who can be called upon to help you to deal with insecurities from the past or present. Zagzagel can give you the wisdom and self-esteem to think positively about the future.

RAPHAEL—THE ANGEL OF HEALING

Call upon the Archangel Raphael (see page 44) for all types of healing, both for yourself and for others. When invoking him, visualize breathing in his Green Ray (see page 107) for self-healing. If sending out healing to others, visualize this Green Ray connecting with them, infusing them with its healing energy.

Moving on with your life

It is sometimes very hard to get on with our lives when we have feelings that attach us to the past, or to other people. We need to call upon the Archangel Michael (see page 42) to help us cut the psychic ties that bind us to events, times, places, and relationships. We may also need to cut our emotional ties with someone trying to control our lives—it could be a partner, colleague, or parent. Throughout our lives, we bond emotionally with numerous people. This is great while a relationship is on an even footing, but if it breaks down you may feel that you cannot get on with your life because this person still has a hold over you. You may also realize that certain people tend to make you feel depressed, negative, or drained when you are in contact with them.

In the "Break free from negativity" exercise on page 134, you will connect with the Archangel Michael, who can help you to cut these ties, allowing you to clear the clutter of negative influences. This may include unwanted aspects of yourself that you know are not healthy, or a fear deeply rooted within your psyche that rears its ugly head every now and then.

BREAK FREE FROM NEGATIVITY

Connect with the Archangel Michael to help break unhealthy emotional ties. Many people visualize him wearing a cobalt blue cloak and carrying a sword, either metal or a flame.

1. Go to a quiet place where you will not be disturbed, or to your sacred space (see page 76). Remove your shoes and place your feet firmly on the floor. Relax; close your eyes.

2. Concentrate on your breathing. Breathe in for a count of four through your nose, then exhale through your mouth for a count of four. Visualize roots growing down through the ground from the soles of your feet. As you breathe, they are probing deeper and deeper, anchoring you to the ground. As you breathe in, visualize inhaling the Blue Ray of the Archangel Michael (see page 105), and as you exhale, visualize expelling any negative thoughts.

3. When you are ready, invoke the Archangel Michael to be with you. Try to feel his presence—be aware of perhaps a slight tingle in your arms, a slight brush against your arm, or a comforting feeling of warmth.

4. Now appeal to him to cover you with his protective cloak, so that nothing can harm you. Imagine this cloak covering you. It may feel solid or it could be light like a cloud—this is your meditation, so whatever feels right for you.

5. Think about the negative influences in your life and ask Archangel Michael to cut the cords that are binding them to you. Visualize a cord reaching from within you, connecting to whatever is holding you back. Visualize him taking his sword and cutting through the cord to set you free. Feel that he has cut away the darkness, negativity, and perhaps fear that has been holding you back and preventing you from getting on with your life.

6. *Now that the negative influences are cut away, ask Michael to help you grow emotionally, physically, and spiritually stronger. Ask him to guide you to have love, patience, and wisdom to deal with new people and situations that are in your life. Remain constantly aware of his cloak around you. Ask the Archangel Michael if he has anything that he would like to tell you.*

7. *When you feel ready, thank the Archangel Michael and visualize his cloak being removed from around you. Concentrate again on your breathing. Visualize the Blue Ray of the Archangel Michael vaporize with each outgoing breath. Be aware of the roots that grew out of the soles of your feet retracting back into the ground.*

8. *Become aware of your physical body; when you feel ready, open your eyes. Take a moment to become fully aware of your surroundings.*

ANGELS AND DEATH

Angels frequently appear to those who are dying in order to ease their passing from this life. One woman told me the following story.

"My mother, it has to be said, was an extremely difficult and unhappy person. When we gathered around her deathbed, a radiant smile illuminated her whole face. I must admit that this was probably the happiest I can remember her looking for many years. She was looking into the corner of the room and her gaze stayed there; it was obvious she was looking at something that was making her very, very happy. As a Christian, I am completely convinced that she saw her guardian angel who had come to help ease her transition over to the other side."

When my aunt was dying, I was there every day with my parents as she slipped into semiconsciousness. During the last two days, there were many times when she was talking lucidly to all her sisters and brothers who had died before her as if they were alive and helping her to make her dying easier. On the last day, I believe that she also talked with her angels, whom she could see, and who were gently easing her through her transition from this world and into the next.

When your time is not up

We are here on Earth to learn lessons to help our souls evolve along their spiritual pathway. Our guardian angel is alongside us, nudging us along our predestined path. However, as we are human and have free choice, we sometimes wander inadvertently away from our destiny. This can lead us to a situation where we are in danger of dying before our pre-allotted time, so our angels have to work overtime to try to make themselves heard in order to save us from mortal danger. This is what happened when angels physically interceded in my mother's life, and in turn in my life.

During 1941 when the German Luftwaffe were regularly bombing London, my mother was traveling home from work on the London Underground. The flat that she was living in was almost opposite Warren Street tube station, in central London, but on this particular occasion she missed her stop and found herself at the next station, Goodge Street, which is about two minutes away. As the train slowed down and pulled into the station, she was aware of a bomb blast in the vicinity. Warren Street tube station had suffered a direct hit, and everyone who had disembarked from the train that my mother was on had been killed. If she had not missed her normal station stop, she would have been killed instantly. My father, who was at that time an air raid warden, knew that my mother was due on that train and heard the bomb go off. He rushed over to the disaster area to look for her.

To this day, my mother is convinced that it was her guardian angel who had protected her. There had been no identifiable reason why she had missed her usual stop. She had never done it before, and it never happened again. One minute she was aware of approaching Warren Street station and thinking about preparing to get off, and the very next moment she realized that she had missed the station and was nearly at the next one, Goodge Street. It was as if time had just moved on without her being aware of it.

My father always taught me that time is an extension, as well as an expression, of the mind. If you pick up a book, you can open it at the beginning, the middle, or the end; so it is with our lives. Although we are aware of living in the present, our future and its impact on humanity is already set along the timeline of the world.

At times of illness

During times of illness, our angels are working overtime to help us to recover. Equally, angels appearing near the dying may symbolize the passing on of the soul. Whatever the circumstance may be, angels very often do appear to guide a person back to health, if it is not their destiny to pass on. However, they may appear to shepherd his or her soul onward, depending on that person's destiny. In the following story, my father's guardian angel brought with him the spirit of a family member, who at that time was unknown to him, and who physically performed hands-on healing. Here is my account of his recovery.

When my father was young, he was very seriously ill with sunstroke. As he lay in a darkened room, he saw a vision of

ANGELS AND MEDICATIONS

You can ask your angels to "charge," or energize, any kind of medication, including vitamins, minerals, or herbs, in order to help with healing. Hold whatever medication you are taking and invoke your angels. Visualize that they are pouring healing and energizing light into the contents, so that they will combine harmoniously with your body.

a beautiful white glowing angel at the bottom of his bed. His angel smiled at him, then a man appeared and came over to him as he lay on the bed and massaged him with some ointment. Both the angel and the man vanished. Somehow, by the evening my father had made a near recovery and when his mother seemed surprised, he told her that an angel had appeared and brought with him a man who had massaged his limbs and made him better. When questioned, he described the man, and his mother looked shocked. She told him that he had described her father, who had passed away many years before my father had been born.

ASKING YOUR ANGELS TO HELP OTHERS

When you pass a hospital, ask your angels to help those inside recover. By directly asking your angels to intervene, you allow them to be more effective in using their healing energies.

If a person dies suddenly, sometimes their souls can feel very lost and do not immediately rise up to the source (heaven). Take a moment to ask your angels to help lead these lost souls to heaven so that they can be at rest.

Animals can also be helped by angels. Visualize the animal in question, and ask your angels to help speed the animal's recovery.

ASKING YOUR ANGELS TO HELP WITH HEALING

1. Sit or lie down comfortably and concentrate on your breathing. Inhale deeply, and then exhale. When you feel truly relaxed, begin to sense the presence of your angels.

2. As you inhale, visualize that you are breathing in a white light of pure energy, which filters through every part of your body.

3. As you exhale, visualize that you are clearing out any blockages that lie within you.

4. Now ask your angels to fill you with their healing energies. If there is something in particular that you need healed, now is the time to ask.

5. Keep breathing, and feel your angels working on you.

6. If there is someone whom you would like your angels to help, picture that person now and visualize your angels working with the white light of their energy and showering that person with their love and care.

7. When you are ready, concentrate on your breathing again and allow the white light of pure energy to leave your body.

8. Thank your angels for all that you have received and for their help. Open your eyes.

When bad news strikes

We can feel enveloped by bad tidings from the media on a daily basis. The next time that you read, see, or hear bad news, take a moment to ask your angels to send some of their healing light and energy to the area. The fact that you are sending out this message helps build an invisible bridge of light along which the angels can direct their energies. The following are examples of such circumstances.

- **Areas of catastrophe (either natural or caused):** Ask your angels to protect, heal, and love those who are involved. Where death has occurred, ask your angels to help those who have suddenly and unexpectedly died to "find the light" as quickly as possible.
- **War zones:** Do not focus on the terrible things that are happening there, but picture angelic light and energy penetrating every part of the area and its surroundings.
- **Perpetrators of evil:** Ask your angels to send love and light to those who abuse the rights of others.

Angel messages

Our angels try to help save us from ourselves—choose to love life and be open to receiving angelic love and heavenly peace.

Life is perpetual and can be filled with joy, but it is up to you to live it this way.

You are never alone. From the moment you were set upon this earth, your guardian angel has been your faithful and loving companion, trying to protect you from any pitfalls in your path.

Let your angels help you to experience the richness and meaningfulness of life!

Knowing my angels has completely changed the way I see the world around me.

Many a time I feel heavy with despair, but as soon as my angels surround me with their sublime energy, the load lightens and then fades away.